IN THIS EDITION ONLY

The complete, in-depth, eyewitness record of the days of terror and tragedy the world will never forget.

Jonestown, Nov. 17

Someone asked Jones about the beatings... this prompted another rage, and I almost felt sorry for the man. "All I want is peace," he raged. "If we could just stop it, stop all this fighting. But if we don't, I don't know what's going to happen to 1,200 lives here..."

Port Kaituma, Nov. 18

I lay there, hoping they'd think I was dead. Suddenly, my left hip burned. I felt a part of a tooth chip, and I knew I'd been hit...

Jonestown, Nov. 20

More than 390 of the bodies were grouped around the altar, many of them arm-in-arm. They were so thickly bunched together that it was impossible to see the ground under them...

Dateline: Guyana
Charles A. Krause

GUYANA MASSACRE: the correspondent and the photographer who lived through it—

CHARLES A. KRAUSE, 31, joined THE WASHINGTON POST as a metropolitan reporter in 1972, after graduating from Princeton University. He covered local and state news for the paper's Maryland desk, and served as Assistant City Editor, before assuming his present position as Latin American Correspondent in 1978.

FRANK JOHNSTON traveled for five years with UPI, including 13 months as Staff Combat Photographer in Vietnam, before joining THE WASHINGTON POST in 1968. He is twice winner of the White House News Photographers Award.

GUYANA MASSACRE: the award-winning
national newsteam who put it *on record*—

LAURENCE M. STERN, 49, is Assistant
Managing Editor (National Affairs) of THE
WASHINGTON POST. He was the chief of the
Saigon Bureau during the Vietnam War, and is
the author of *The Wrong Horse*, a study of
American foreign policy.

RICHARD HARWOOD, Deputy Managing
Editor, came to THE WASHINGTON POST in
1966 from the Louisville (Ky.) COURIER-
JOURNAL. A journalist for 30 years, he has
covered both Kennedy assassinations, the killings
at Kent State, and the Vietnam War.

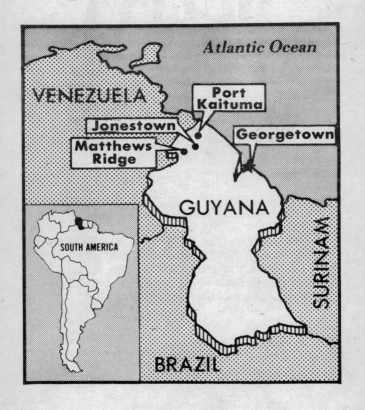

GUYANA MASSACRE

THE EYEWITNESS ACCOUNT

CHARLES A. KRAUSE

WITH EXCLUSIVE MATERIAL BY

Laurence M. Stern, Richard Harwood

AND THE STAFF OF

The Washington Post

With 16 pages of on-the-scene photographs
and commentary by Frank Johnston

A BERKLEY BOOK
published by
BERKLEY PUBLISHING CORPORATION

Berkley Publishing Corporation
200 Madison Avenue
New York, New York 10016

SBN 425-04234-0

*BERKLEY BOOKS are published by
Berkley Publishing Corporation*

BERKLEY BOOK ® TM 757,375

Printed in the United States of America

Berkley Edition, DECEMBER, 1978

ACKNOWLEDGMENTS

In addition to the eyewitness account by Charles A. Krause and the narrative written by Laurence M. Stern and Richard Harwood, special appreciation is due the work of Jane E. Freundel for research and editing of the manuscript; to photographer Frank Johnston, whose photographs are central to the special photo section; and to correspondents Leonard Downie, Jr., Karen DeYoung and Fred Barbash, who joined Krause in Guyana as the story unfolded.

Among those responsible for editing and directing the coverage in the hectic hours following word of the murder of Representative Ryan and others were: managing editor Howard Simons; assistant managing editor Philip Foisie; foreign editor Peter Osnos; deputy foreign editor Jay Ross; and assistant foreign editors Richard M. Weintraub, Terri Shaw, Joe Ritchie, and Lexie Verdon.

Assisting from the national staff: assistant national editor Peter Masley, Western bureau chief Lou Cannon; special correspondents Joel Kotkin, Paul Grabowicz, Francis Moriarity, Bill Wallace, Hal Lipper, and John Jacobs; staff writers Art Harris, Larry Kramer, T. R. Reid, John Goshko, Karlyn Barker, and Henry Allen; and assistant national editors Larry Fox, Robin D. Meszoly, and Joel R. Garreau.

William B. Dickinson, general manager of *The Washington Post* Writers Group, was responsible for publishing coordination in cooperation with Executive Editor Benjamin C. Bradlee.

CONTENTS

For my family, my friends, and my colleagues at *The Post* whose thoughts and prayers were with me during a long, terrifying night.

1.

"An unbelievable story."

I remember thinking, this is crazy. It couldn't be. I was going to die in the middle of the jungle of Guyana, far away from my family and friends.

We were in the process of boarding two small planes at Port Kaituma's jungle landing strip, nearing the end of a curious story about a Congressman who wanted to investigate a freaky religious commune in Guyana. Suddenly the story was no longer zany. Three men on a dump truck and tractor approached our aircraft and began shooting. I went down.

The bodies of other passengers started rolling over me as the shooting intensified. The shots were louder—and closer. I could feel dirt spraying over me but I didn't hear anyone screaming or moaning. Just the pop-pop-pop of the bullets.

I lay behind one of the wheels of the plane, hoping they would think I was dead. I knew then I was in the wrong place because they had come around to my side of the plane. Suddenly, my left hip burned. I felt a part of a tooth chip, and I knew I had been hit. I was

1

helpless. I thought that I wanted to be home. I was waiting to die and, as the seconds went by, I became resigned. O.K., I was ready.

Then the shots seemed to come from further away. I don't know how long the assault lasted—maybe five minutes. I finally got up and it was clear that the expedition led by Congressman Leo J. Ryan of California to the Peoples Temple commune at Jonestown in the Guyana jungle had ended in tragedy. It would escalate in the next few hours and become one of the most bizarre and awful massacres of our time.

When it was over, more than 900 Jonestown people would be dead and rotting in the blistering heat of a tropical rain forest. They were babies and school kids, old men and women, most of them innocent Americans who had sought a Utopian society thousands of miles from the ghettoes, from the crime, the drugs, and the failure that had been their lot before. They had been led to Guyana by a messianic fundamentalist preacher whose faith-healing, old-time religion and sophisticated Marxist philosophy attracted to him unlettered blacks, whites from the Okie migrations to California in the 1930s, and cadres of alienated young people—black and white—who despaired of creating in the United States the inter-racial socialist society they longed for. The preacher was Jim Jones, who was called "Father" by his flock; he had built a small religious order in Ukaiah, California, into an influential political institution that was to flower and be destroyed in the Guyana jungle.

Whatever his messianic appeal, whatever his high-minded idealism, whatever his good works and his effort to build God's kingdom on earth, he will be remembered now as an insane and tragic man. He saw himself as a reincarnation of Christ and Lenin. In death, he more resembles Lucifer.

I had never heard of Jim Jones until a few days before the holocaust and even then it was almost by accident. It began in the Tamanaco Intercontinental Hotel in Caracas.

I was in Venezuela to cover the national elections as a correspondent for *The Washington Post*. I had been living in South America for eight months and it had been an exhausting time. There had been coups in Bolivia, elections in Peru and Ecuador, difficult dealings with dictatorships in Argentina, Chile, and Uruguay, and a curious interview with the survivors of an Andes air crash whose book, *Alive*, described their survival on the flesh of dead companions. There also had been the long days of boredom and frustration that mark the lives of all correspondents.

In Caracas, I looked forward to the next few days when I would be heading home for a Thanksgiving Day reunion with my family and friends. It was to be my first trip back to the states since March.

Then came the telephone call that was to involve me with Jim Jones and almost cost me my life.

The caller was *The Post*'s foreign editor, Peter Osnos. He told me about a delegation that was headed for Guyana to investigate the Peoples Temple and Jim Jones. Osnos, like me, knew nothing about Jones. But he thought it might be an interesting, off-beat story. The head of the delegation, Representative Ryan, was a Bay Area liberal who had spent six years in relative anonymity in Washington. His party included several journalists from California and a television crew from NBC News.

Osnos wanted me to leave the next day and hook up with the Ryan group in Georgetown, Guyana. He thought I might have trouble getting in because of visa problems, but that I ought to try.

My reaction was not entirely positive. I had only been in Venezuela for 24 hours and that was insufficient time to do a decent job on the upcoming election. Beyond that, the "religious cult" phenomenon had never appealed to me as a story. But I was interested in getting to Guyana for the first time and the story did have the possibility of getting more attention in the paper than some of my recent offerings on Latin American affairs.

We agreed that night—November 13—that I would make the necessary travel arrangements. I went off to dinner with another correspondent and the next day found out I could meet Ryan and his party in Trinidad. We hooked up that night in the Trinidad airport where I met for the first time the people who were going to be involved (in ways they could not imagine) in events that lay ahead. Some of them had less than a week to live—Ryan; Don Harris, an NBC correspondent; Bob Brown, an NBC cameraman; and Greg Robinson, a photographer for the *San Francisco Examiner*. I also met that night Tim Stoen, a San Francisco lawyer who had once been among the most trusted lieutenants of the Reverend Jim Jones. He was now a leader of a group that had come along with Ryan to persuade their relatives to abandon Jonestown and return from the jungle to their homes in California.

Enroute from Trinidad to Georgetown, Stoen gave me a thick file of affidavits, news stories and press releases detailing what seemed to me then an unbelievable story of physical abuse and psychological terror in Jim Jones's Utopian community. If true, we were heading into a jungle Gulag. I was so skeptical I thought Stoen was crazy.

Congressman Ryan had not reached a decision on Stoen's heavy indictment of the Jones cult. But he was sufficiently concerned about the complaints and fears of other relatives—some of them on the plane—that he had received authorization from the House International Affairs Committee to make an official inquiry by the U.S. government. He made no secret of his feeling that the State Department in Washington and the U.S. Embassy in Georgetown had done little to get at the truth.

I was the only journalist aboard who was not based in California. The others were a fraternity apart. They seemed to know all about Jones and his Temple and Leo Ryan and his political situation. I was the outsider. Only Jackie Speier, Ryan's legislative assistant, and Jim Schollaert, of the International Affairs Committee staff, were friendly and helpful. They were impressed with *The Washington Post* and its interest in the story and were anxious that Ryan shouldn't come through as a junketeering Don Quixote in whatever was written.

The flight from Trinidad took only an hour. It was a little after midnight on November 15 when we landed at Georgetown's Timehri Airport. It was hot and muggy and I was tired. I didn't know what would come out of this strange trip and didn't particularly care. I just wanted to go to bed.

2.

LEO J. RYAN:
His Own Drummer

"Leave it alone," Congressman Don Edwards warned his friend and colleague, Leo J. Ryan, in declining an invitation to join Ryan on his mission to Guyana. "Don't mess around with those people. Those cultists are all crazy."

But for most of his four-term Congressional career the 53-year-old Ryan had been "messing around"— investigating whatever piqued his insatiable curiosity or sense of political theater. When Watts in Los Angeles exploded in the summer of 1965 Ryan moved into the area, taking up residence with a black family, and started working as a substitute teacher under an assumed name. He was at the time a California state legislator, but he wanted to understand the causes of the riot at first hand.

The same year he made a trip to Newfoundland to denounce the hunting of harp seal pups. He was promptly proclaimed the International Wildlife Foundation's "Man of the Year." In 1970 he had himself taken in handcuffs and leg irons under an assumed identity to spend eight days at Folsom Prison investigating reports of abuses in the California penal institution and wrote an

unpublished play on the experience. "The greatest thing I
learned there was not to be afraid any more," he told
friends.

Tall, silver-haired, a politician with an adroit gift for
attracting headlines and television lenses, Ryan had
always managed to draw attention to his feisty crusades.
In the House, he had a reputation for mercurial,
sometimes abrasive, behavior. In the clubby ambience of
Congress, Ryan was something of a loner. "Leo went very
much to his own drummer," said his friend, Representative Fortney H. (Pete) Stark. It seemed somehow
appropriate that Ryan was the member of Congress
whose district included Hillsborough, Patty Hearst's
family home. For it was inevitably Ryan who led the
campaign in Congress for the commutation of Patty
Hearst's sentence with a letter to Attorney General Griffin
Bell signed by 48 other members of the House. Before
launching the campaign, he conferred with his famous
constituent in a well-publicized *tête-à-tête* at the Federal
Penitentiary at Pleasanton, California.

By the standards of both Congressional and California
politics Leo Ryan was on the left liberal side of the
political spectrum, ranking with such fellow Californians
as Edwards, and Representatives Phillip Burton and Pete
Stark. Yet he could rally to the defense of such a pillar of
the political establishment as former Representative
Wayne Hays during the Congressional sex-and-payroll
scandals of two years ago. Unlike some of his California
colleagues, Ryan loudly denounced South Korean
President Park Chung Hee whose agents had spread
money and other blandishments to members of the
House. Ryan loudly rejected an honorary Korean
university doctoral degree and the accompanying
expense-paid, fun-filled trip to Korea. When crossed,
Ryan could be impetuous and unforgiving. Handed a $5
parking ticket at a Sacramento airport on December 7,
1976, he demanded a jury trial and intimated that he
might restrict revenue-sharing funds for the state capital.

This was the man who led the fateful mission to
Jonestown, Guyana, on Friday, November 17—a
stubborn, restlessly curious, publicity-conscious figure

who saw himself in political and public relations terms as Congressional knight-errant, a righter of wrongs.

"I asked him if it wasn't dangerous," Ryan's 80-year-old mother, Autumn Mead Ryan, said after the jungle holocaust in Jonestown. "His reply was that lots of things in life are a risk ... Leo told me that he had received at least 100 letters from people warning him not to go, asking him not to investigate the Peoples Temple. I had a gut feeling that this was a dangerous, emotional, undisciplined cult. I cautioned him to be very careful.

"Leo said he could not do his job if he gave in to fear. So he put fear aside."

Ryan's administrative assistant, Galen W. Holsinger, was also among those who told the Congressman of his keen misgivings about the trip to Jonestown. "I'm not a very religious man, but I found myself getting down on my knees Friday night and praying for Leo's safety. These people were crazy and dangerous," Holsinger recalled afterward.

The saga that ended for Ryan with bloody finality on Port Kaituma airstrip in Guyana started in the late summer of 1977 in the living room of an old friend, Sam Houston, an Associated Press photographer. Speaking with difficulty because of his cancer-choked larynx, Houston told Ryan an eerie story of how his son, Robert Houston, Jr., his daughter-in-law, and two grandchildren had joined the Peoples Temple cult in San Francisco.

Bob, Jr., an intelligent young man who Ryan had once taught in high school, worked as a probation officer by day and a railroad worker by night in order to be able to turn over as much as $2000 a month to the church. Dedicated as he was to Reverend Jones and his Temple, young Houston would openly argue his differences with the cult ideology and, in reprisal, was subjected to harsh punishment ordered by the leader.

On the morning of October 5, 1976, Houston learned that his son, then 33, had been found mangled along the railroad tracks where he had worked. How this bizarre accident happened was never explained to the family's satisfaction.

From the account of the father and other breakaway

members of the cult, the *San Francisco Examiner* learned
the gruesome details of young Houston's ordeal during
his period of service to the Peoples Temple. On one
occasion he had been beaten bloody by another church
member in front of the congregation as punishment for
questioning points of doctrine. During these punishments
resistance was forbidden. Although Houston was holding
down two jobs and showering the proceeds into the
Temple's coffers, Reverend Jones scathingly branded him
a "narcoleptic" for falling asleep during the all-night
temple meetings.

"I just can't understand how my son, bright as he was,
could be taken in by a thing like this. It must be like a
cancer," Ryan's friend, Sam Houston, mused to a
reporter afterward. "It grows slowly and takes a long time
to come to a head." His two grandchildren were last heard
from in the Guyana encampment at Jonestown.

As Ryan pressed his investigation, he heard from more
of the divided families with relatives in thrall to Jones and
his cult. An organization called "Concerned Relatives"
provided more and more details of the bizarre practices of
the Peoples Temple. The long-suppressed secret abuses of
the congregation and growing propensity toward violence
were first publicly chronicled in the magazine *New
West*—giving the first significant impetus to critics of the
California cult leader.

Ryan pressed his inquiries with the Department of
State and other agencies which might have information
on the cult, its leadership, and its constituent-victims.
After the assassination in Guyana, friends and associates
of Ryan would comment bitterly that his death and the
ensuing mass suicides might have been avoided—that all
were casualties of the failure by U.S. authorities to
investigate and report adequately on the conditions in the
Guyana colony.

American consular officials in Guyana had visited the
commune four times during 1978, the last occasion was
on November 7, eleven days before the massacre. Each
time, according to State Department sources, the officials
privately interviewed cult members who had been

described in complaints from relatives as being held against their will. "More than 75 Temple members talked to our consular officers over the last year and not one confirmed any allegation of mistreatment," Deputy Assistant Secretary of State for Inter-American Affairs John A. Bushnell announced to reporters after the mass death.

The State Department held a series of briefings for Ryan, Bushnell said, and warned the Congressman that the Jonestown commune had armed guards, that it was in a remote jungle area with "no significant law enforcement presence," and that the powers of the U.S. Embassy in Georgetown, 150 miles away, were very limited in the degree of protection it could provide to the visiting party.

At the same time, the State Department had been describing conditions at the colony to worried relatives in words of almost rosy reassurance. A form letter the Department sent inquiring relatives told them that American consular officers visited the encampment regularly.

"It is the opinion of these officers," the U.S. Government communication said, "reinforced by conversations with local officials, who deal with the Peoples Temple, that it is improbable anyone is being held in bondage. In general the people appear healthy, adequately fed and housed, and satisfied with their lives on what is a large farm. Many do hard physical labor, but there is no evidence of persons being forced to work beyond their capacity or against their will."

The beatings, the grisly solitary confinements, and the forced labor punishment which surfaced fully in the later accounts of those who escaped to corroborate earlier fragmentary reports eluded the attention of the State Department monitors. This is not surprising. The U.S. mission in Guyana was small and overworked. There were only two consular officers to handle the work of the embassy and to make the arduous air trip to Jonestown. Reverend Jones and his chief followers were highly talented political cosmeticians who could arrange their Potemkin village to dazzle the credulity of any visitor,

however skeptical. That hard-pressed consular officials
from Georgetown should come away with a view of
Jonestown as a jungle Arcadia was perhaps a pardonable
bureaucratic reporting lapse.

At the time of Ryan's last briefing, September 15, the
Inter-American Bureau of the State Department was
absorbed by the bloody civil war in Nicaragua. It could
hardly be expected to pay full time and attention to an
American cult in the jungles of Guyana.

Ryan was also having his troubles with the Reverend
Jim Jones and his attorney, Mark Lane, in setting up the
visit to the Peoples Temple in Jonestown. On November
1st, he wired Reverend Jones that "I am most interested in
a visit to Jonestown, and would appreciate whatever
courtesies you can extend to our Congressional delegation." Ryan explained in the wire that he had been visited
by constituents "who expressed anxiety about mothers
and fathers, sons and daughters, brothers and sisters who
have elected to assist you in the development of your
church in Guyana."

He heard back in a week from Mark Lane, writing in
behalf of Reverend Jones. Lane insisted that he be present
during the negotiations, although he said that the
Congressional delegation would be welcome in Jonestown. The Lane letter also spoke of "religious persecution"
and governmental "witch hunts" against the church. "You
may judge, therefore, the important consequences which
may flow from further persecution of Peoples Temple and
which might very well result in the creation of a most
embarrassing situation for the U.S. Government," Lane
warned.

Ryan wrote Lane back that he intended to go ahead
with his trip as scheduled and acidly observed: "No
'persecution,' as you put it, is intended, Mr. Lane. But
your vague reference to the 'creation of the most
embarrassing situation for the American government'
does not impress me at all."

It was a fittingly acrimonious beginning.

3.

"These people were crazy."

A few minutes after midnight on Wednesday, November 15, Congressman Leo Ryan and two staff assistants—Jackie Speier and Jim Schollaert—were given the VIP treatment by Guyanese immigration officials at the Georgetown airport. They moved quickly through the gates, were met by U.S. Embassy officials, and were driven off in official cars to Guyana's capital city, a somnolent, overgrown village an hour's drive from the airport. Ryan was to stay in Ambassador John Burke's residence, enroute to his death in the jungle less than 72 hours later. Speier and Schollaert had rooms waiting for them at the Pegasus Hotel in Georgetown.

The rest of us—nine journalists and 13 members of the Concerned Relatives group—stood for an hour in the airport—sweating, hot, and tired—waiting in long lines to be processed by customs and immigration. The air in the terminal was stale and humid. I thought it was a fitting introduction to Guyana and to the kooky assignment that had brought me here.

Two members of Jim Jones's Peoples Temple were at the airport to watch our arrival. They caused a stir among the Californians. One of the Templeites was Sherwin Harris's ex-wife Linda, who was now known as Sharon. She ignored her former husband and stared silently as we moved slowly through the lines. Four days later, she would be dead, her throat slashed. The Harris's 22-year-old daughter, Liane, would die, too, as a side event to the massacre that was coming.

I had no intimations of any of that. This story was starting out as a tedious farce, peopled with crazies and publicity hounds. All I wanted was to get my passport stamped and head for the Pegasus Hotel, where I assumed I had a room reserved and waiting.

The first bureaucratic hitch of the night came when Ron Javers, a reporter for the *San Francisco Chronicle*, was detained by one of the immigration officers. Two days later, Javers would be lying on a jungle tarmac with a bullet in his shoulder. On this night, he had other problems. He was questioned extensively and then taken to a passenger lounge on the second story of the airport. He was told he would not be allowed to enter Guyana.

I was damned if I was going to have the same problem, after coming this far. I quickly wrote down my name on a piece of paper and handed it to one of the Concerned Relatives standing in line behind me. If they don't let me through, I told the woman, call the U.S. Embassy as soon as you get to Georgetown. Tell them, I told her, to get someone from the embassy to the airport immediately. I promised myself that *The Washington Post* is not going to spend the night in a crummy airport and then be shipped out on the first plane back to Trinidad. I didn't have any great zest for this story, but if this was going to be a test, *The Post* was going to win.

When my turn with immigration came, my shirt was soaked with sweat. I was asked why I wanted to enter Guyana and I came up with a deceptive answer: I was the South American correspondent for

my newspaper and I had two interests in Guyana—
the political situation in this small, former British
colony and, well, yes, I did plan to cover the
congressman's visit to Jonestown.

That deception had a point. We had been told that
the Reverend Jim Jones seemed to have a lot of clout
with the Guyanese government. Once before he had
succeeded in barring from the country Gordon
Lindsay, one of the journalists who was on this trip
with Ryan.

I don't think the immigration official was fooled by
my answer. But after a conference with another
official he said I would get a 24-hour visa that would
have to be extended the next day if I wanted to
remain in Guyana. The other journalists got the
same treatment, except for Javers, who was still
being detained upstairs.

I didn't argue. At least I wouldn't have to spend the
night at the airport and would be in the same boat as
the others. I figured if the Guyanese government
decided to throw representatives of *The Washington
Post*, NBC, and the San Francisco papers out of the
country, that would be a good story, maybe a better
story than this garbage about the Peoples Temple.
Javers, in fact, already had a story: although he was
to be allowed in at noon, 12 hours after the plane
landed, he wrote a first person account of his
detention that the *San Francisco Chronicle* carried
on its front page that day.

Free at last, I headed for Georgetown and the
Pegasus Hotel in a cab shared with three Guyanese
who had nothing to do with the Ryan mission. They
didn't tell me anything about Jonestown but I did
learn that it's not safe to walk the streets of
Georgetown day or night. They said thieves, using a
technique they call "choke and rob" and I call
mugging, were all over the city, waiting to steal
rings, watches, money, or anything else of value. We
would all have been lucky if a mugging was the worst
thing that came out of this trip.

At the hotel, there was another foul up. The other

members of Ryan's party were crowded around the reception desks, their luggage piled up in the unimpressive lobby. The desk clerk was apologetic. Our rooms had been given away to other guests. The Concerned Relatives thought this was part of a plot by the Peoples Temple to discourage their visit. I thought it was just another irritating episode in the farce. It was 2:30 A.M. All I wanted was a bed. The thought of spending the night on the lobby floor with a bunch of crazy "relatives" and unfriendly reporters was depressing.

I tried to make the best of it and decided to talk to some of the "relatives" since I had only the vaguest idea what this story was supposed to be about.

I picked out Sherwin Harris because he was wearing an intriguing ornament around his neck—a Star of David. How could a Jew be involved in a Christian church?

Harris told me a long, sad story and, long before he was finished I decided that being a Jew and being involved with this strange cult was as logical and consistent as anything else I had heard. Nothing made any sense: Jones, Jonestown, the Peoples Temple back in San Francisco, and, most especially, this group of relatives, many of them former Temple members, who seemed nice enough, even if a little crazy. The things they were saying—that Jonestown was a concentration camp and Jones the reincarnation, not of Lenin and Jesus Christ, but of Himmler—seemed preposterous.

Harris had never joined the Temple. But he had not resisted when his ex-wife, Linda, and his daughter, Liane, had joined 10 years before. He got worried, he said, only a couple of years ago when Liane drifted further and further away from him as she got more and more involved in the Temple.

But after 20 years of his life story, I was convinced that Liane had simply grown up and decided her father was a jerk. He told me he had divorced Liane's mother when the child was less than two years old, had had a second wife from whom he was now divorced, and was living with another woman somewhere in the Bay area. Sherwin wouldn't tell me where they lived. He said he was afraid the Jonestown people might try to track him down and kill him.

The next of these Canterbury tales came from Grace Stoen, an attractive woman in her mid-twenties who was once, along with her husband, Tim, a leading spear carrier in the Peoples Temple hierarchy. She claimed to have witnessed many scenes of horror in the church: all-night meetings presided over by Jones, paddlings and other crude forms of punishment in the presence of the congregation. She described Jones's technique of turning his followers against each other by sowing mistrust and fear. Finally, she told me the complicated and ultimately unbelievable story of John-John Stoen, Grace's six-year-old son. As she talked that night, John-John had three days to live.

Tim Stoen, Grace told me, had signed an affidavit saying that John-John's natural father was Jim Jones. Tim had also signed a legal document giving custody of John-John to Jones, who had taken the boy to Jonestown and kept him there for over a year. Grace and Tim were now claiming that Tim really was John-John's natural father and that they had gotten a court order in California, ordering Jones to turn the child over to Grace. I didn't know that night that a year earlier Jones had threatened a mass suicide of Temple members if John-John were taken from him. And if I had known it, I wouldn't have believed it.

As the long night dragged on, I thought the Stoens's story was one of the unlikeliest I had ever heard.

Here was Grace Stoen proudly admitting that her husband, Tim, a practicing lawyer and graduate of Stanford Law School, had signed phony legal documents as an "act of faith" when he was a

member of the Peoples Temple and a personal legal
advisor to Jones. It was beyond my comprehension
that a man with Stoen's credentials could have
signed such documents.

And for Tim Stoen to now claim that he loved the
child, that Jones was not John-John's father, and
that he and Grace, who were now divorced, wanted
their son back was too much. I was more firmly
convinced than ever that this weird assortment of
people in the lobby of the Pegasus were the crazy
ones, that Jim Jones with his 900 or more followers
had to be, sight unseen, the victim of raging
paranoia by this group of California crazies.

I'd had enough of strange stories. It was 3:30 A.M.
and I needed sleep. Luckily, someone discovered at
that godawful hour that there was another hotel in
Georgetown with rooms available. I took off in the
company of four of the women "relatives" and we
checked in to the Tower Hotel.

The next morning, at about 10 o'clock, a Mr. Ellis
from the U.S. Embassy woke me with a telephone
call. He said reporter Javers was still at the airport,
that some of the other journalists at the Pegasus had
already gone to the Home Affairs Ministry to extend
their visas and he advised me to do the same if I
wanted to stay in Guyana.

I got over to the Ministry quickly and had my first
encounter with Comrade Beird. He was chief of
security at the Ministry, a young, very tall black man
who was friendly enough but noncommital about
the visa question. He took my name and passport
number and asked me a few questions about the
purpose of my visit. He told me to come back to his
office after the lunch hour. I noticed that he had
copies of the 1976 and 1977 yearbooks of Novosti, a
news agency in the Soviet Union. I didn't know the
significance of that, if any, but the thought occurred
to me that he might check me out as a potential CIA
agent. The Guyanese government, like the Jones
Temple, had Marxist leanings and close ties with

China, the U.S.S.R., and Cuba. Americans were suspect.

I left the Comrade's office and stopped by the American Embassy to kill time and try to get a briefing on the Reverend Jones and his colony. I met Richard Dwyer, the deputy chief of the mission, learned that Javers had finally been released from the airport, and that our visit—because of Ryan's presence and the presence of the contingent of journalists—was the biggest thing that had happened to the American diplomats in a long time.

But that didn't stop Dwyer and other embassy personnel from heading off at 11:30 A.M. for the weekly luncheon meeting of the Georgetown Rotary Club at the Pegasus Hotel.

I was more convinced than ever that this trip would turn out to be a farce.

The next couple of days in Georgetown confirmed that judgment. There was endless bickering within the group. Ryan manfully tried to hold things together and make everyone happy. He held any number of mini-press conferences for our benefit. He negotiated with the embassy, with the Guyanans, with Jonestown representatives in Georgetown and the factions in his own party. When it seemed that Ryan would be stymied in his efforts to get into the jungle, Don Harris of NBC entered into his own negotiations with the Jonestown people for a trip to the Temple.

I was keeping notes chronologically, a minute-by-minute running account of this developing farce. I had become convinced that there wasn't any story at Jonestown worth our front page. But there was a chance that this scene itself was funny enough to make a good piece. I felt like I was living the real life of the fictional character, Boot, the hero of Evelyn Waugh's comic novel on foreign correspondents in the 1930s. Its title was *Scoop.*

Some of my notes give a flavor of those days:

A lunch the first day with some of the Concerned

Relatives at which Sherwin Harris describes a phone conversation with his ex-wife Linda/Sharon. She accused him of wanting to "destroy us" and he replied: "Hey, I'm in the vending machine business. I don't have time for heavy destruction."

A meeting of the other journalists who were furious that I—the outsider—was the only newsman who had traipsed along with Ryan to an unscheduled appearance at the Georgetown headquarters of the Jonestown colony. I had spent the time at the headquarters cooling my heels in a cab while Ryan spent 40 minutes inside. Nonetheless, the other reporters accused Ryan the next day of favoring the "Eastern press" over the hometown boys.

A media event on Thursday at which U.S. Ambassador John Burke refused to let newsmen attend his meeting with the Concerned Relatives. With the television cameras whirring, they demanded that Burke let the press in. It was the kind of thing that happens in Washington all the time, but in sleepy Georgetown in the heat and the dust, it seemed anachronistic, pointless, and funny.

I wearied of it all and went off to write a piece on the Venezuelan elections.

All this time, however, there were undercurrents of tension and frustration building up in Ryan. He was uncertain he would ever get to Jonestown, in which case his mission would be a failure—in full view of his hometown newspapers, *The Post,* and a national television network.

In addition the Concerned Relatives would be angry because he had failed to get them into Jonestown.

Despite the pressure he was under and my view that most of the Concerned Relatives were paranoid and crazy, Ryan struck me not as a publicity hound but rather as a Congressman deeply troubled by the possibility that Jonestown was at least partly the tropical Gulag its detractors said it was. Jackie Speier explained at one point that one of the

Congressman's nephews had joined the Moonies and that, as a result, Ryan had become suspicious of religious cults in general. The Congressman himself was Catholic.

"The only question that has been raised in my mind (about Jonestown) is whether people have the right to come and go," Ryan said at a meeting with us Thursday morning. He said he could understand and accept the idea that the commune might be run along authoritarian lines. "I can accept that because you can't put 1,200 people in the middle of a jungle without some damn tight discipline."

His mission, Ryan continued, was not to pass judgment on anything other than the right of the Jonestown residents to leave. If they were allowed to leave when they wanted, he would end his inquiry, he said. But if not, as the Concerned Relatives claimed, then Jonestown was a prison, he said, and he would do all he could to expose it.

He ended the meeting by saying: "In the words of John Donne, 'Any man's death diminishes me.' There's a corollary here: 'Any man's diminution of freedom anywhere in the world diminishes freedom everywhere.' " At the time, Ryan's words didn't seem corny, although we were still no closer to Jonestown that Thursday morning than we had been 36 hours before—when we first arrived in Guyana.

The forebodings of failure were intensified with the arrival of a petition from 600 Jonestown colonizers telling Ryan and his entourage to stay away:

"We have not invited and do not care to see Congressman Ryan (supporter of military aid to the Pinochet regime in Chile), media representatives, members of a group of so-called 'Concerned Relatives', or any other persons who may be traveling with, or associated with, any of those persons."

Missing from the list of the petition's signers, were the names of 10 loved ones being sought by the

Concerned Relatives in Ryan's group. This set off much speculation about the fate of the 10. Were they dead? Had they refused to sign as an appeal for help? Nobody knew, but the effect was to raise the level of suspicion, which was already very high. To me, it seemed like more of the paranoia I attributed to the group.

On Thursday, there was a new angle to the story. We learned that Mark Lane and Charles Garry and maybe Dick Gregory were headed for Guyana to represent Bishop Jones and Jonestown in negotiations with Ryan.

They were colorful figures who would finally, I thought, rescue this story from the theater of farce to the theater of the absurd. The last I had heard of Lane, he was in Washington pushing his latest conspiracy theories before the House Assassinations Committee. Garry came with credentials out of the 1960s as the passionate lawyer for the Black Panthers in Oakland. Gregory was a legendary civil rights activist who had given up a professional career as a comedian to take up a professional career as a demonstrator.

The next morning, there was some action. Ryan announced that he was going to Jonestown that day with or without permission and that he would take along the news contingent and some of the Concerned Relatives. He said his plan was to show up at the colony and demand entrance. If that failed, he said, he would at least have tried and be able to say that Jones and his followers had something to hide.

We also learned that morning that Garry and Lane were to be at the hotel at 10:30 A.M. to negotiate with Ryan, who was still hoping for an invitation from Jones. Gregory was not coming.

The two lawyers, in the company of Linda/Sharon Amos, showed up on time. Their encounter with Ryan started out on a sour note. He insisted that the press be present for the negotiations. They refused. Ryan left it to the reporters:

"It's up to you guys."

Most of us didn't care whether the negotiations were conducted in public or in private. Our only concern was to get the show on the road and fly to Jonestown. The upshot was a 30-minute private meeting in a hotel room.

When it ended, Lane and Garry went off to contact Jonestown. They knew Ryan was going there with or without an invitation. They asked him to wait until 2 P.M. and promised to have him an answer from Jonestown by that hour.

That was going to be too late. The logistics involved meant that the chartered airplane (costing $3,000 a day) would not get us to Jonestown until so late in the day that we would have only 15 minutes or so at the Temple before heading back to Georgetown.

We piled into cabs and headed for the airport. We didn't know when we'd be back. Lane and Garry met us at the airport and climbed aboard for the flight to the primitive airstrip at Port Kaituma, a 90-minute drive from Jonestown.

This junket may have been comic up to this point. But comedy or not, my adrenalin was starting to flow. We were headed into the jungle, toward this strange community I had heard so much about.

If I had known what I was getting into, I probably never would have gone. A good story is one thing. But getting killed is another.

Wayne Pietila, one of the Concerned Relatives I met the first night in Georgetown, was not on the plane this day. I guess that was lucky for him, because within 24 hours his stepfather, Tom Kice, Sr., would be shooting at us, trying to kill us as we tried to leave Port Kaituma for the flight back to Georgetown.

But as we set out, leaving about 2:30 P.M. this Friday, November 17, we had no premonition of disaster. We were headed to Jonestown and a meeting with the mysterious Jim Jones.

4.

THE REVEREND JIM JONES:
Father

The Reverend Jim Jones in the final days at his Peoples Temple colony in the Guyana jungle was a figure who might have been wrought by Joseph Conrad. He was the paranoid messiah of a terrorized but devoted congregation whose end he predicted nightly at the hands of dark, encircling forces: the CIA, the Ku Klux Klan, racism, fascism, nuclear holocaust. "Father" he was called by his flock, both in love and in fear. (He chose the salutation himself to evoke deliberately in his followers the memory of the black evangelist, Father Divine.) He professed at times to be the spiritual heir of Christ and/or Lenin. He spouted a doctrine of apostolic socialism while appropriating to his Temple's treasury millions of dollars worth of property, cash, social security and welfare checks of his flock. In the final years of his San Francisco and then Guyanan ministries, Jones proved himself to have been one of the most macabre religious cult figures on the American scene. Had serious national attention been given to his message and early warnings of breakaway members, there might have been more forewarning of the awful denouement that was to come in Guyana and, perhaps, action that might have prevented it.

His was truly a Jekyll-and-Hyde personality. He courted and was courted by powerful California and even national politicians. The congregation at the Peoples Temple was a dedicated political cadre that could write letters, stuff envelopes, get out the vote, cheer, distribute literature, and organize crowds. When Rosalynn Carter came to San Francisco to open the city's Democratic campaign headquarters, Reverend Jones was at her side. When she drew a polite spattering of applause he inspired a thundering roar of enthusiasm from the threats of some 600—all disciples of the Peoples Temple who had been ordered there by Jones.

At the height of his power, state and city political luminaries flocked to his temple, a buff-colored former synagogue in the Fillmore district: Governor Jerry Brown, District Attorney Joe Freitas, Sheriff Richard Hongisto, others. Lieutenant Government Merwyn Dymally made a pilgrimage to Jonestown, the 27,000 acre colony in Guyana, and pronounced it good. In 1975 Jones had turned out a force of 150 precinct workers which was considered crucial in Mayor George Moscone's 4000 vote mayor victory that year. Perhaps in gratitude Moscone named Jones head of the San Francisco Housing Authority. The Peoples Temple lawyer, Tim Stoen, was hired by District Attorney Freitas. Temple members were scattered through the city's bureaucracy. Jones was said virtually to rule the welfare department, able to resolve the benefit problems of his flock with a quick phone call. Welfare and social security checks were an important source of funding for Jones. After the mass suicides in Jonestown on November 18, searchers and rescue workers found piles of uncashed government checks and piles of cash that amounted, according to initial reports, to more than half a million dollars.

Who was Jones? What influences molded him? How did he manage to exercise such a remarkable sway over thousands of followers who heeded his call?

The earliest years of his childhood were the subject of sharply conflicting testimony, just as was the rest of his life.

George Southworth, a University of Miami journalism professor, grew up as a neighbor of the Jones family in the central Indiana town of Lynn. He remembers Jones in childhood as a "mean little six-year-old kid—the Dennis the Menace of Lynn, Indiana." In a remembrance written for the *Miami Herald* after the mass suicide in Guyana, Southworth wrote: "We came to know Jimmy well from the time he was about six years old, because he would walk by our house and shout obscenities... He had special words of endearment for me whenever we met on the street near our homes.

"'Good morning, you son-of-a-bitch,' would be his greeting and then I would chase him because he was about a dozen years my junior. My mother... was always shocked by his language."

The Ku Klux Klan was a strong political force in Lynn and, according to Southworth, Jim Jones's father was a loyal member. "In the 20 years that I lived in Lynn, I saw only one black in the town. There was an unwritten law that blacks should not let the sun set on their heads in Lynn... This was the atmosphere in which Jimmy Jones, the leader of the Peoples Temple, learned about blacks and race relations," Southworth recalled.

The contrasting account comes from a 1953 Richmond, Indiana, newspaper story which shows evidence of having been influenced by Jones. It was the first installment in the lifelong hagiography of the preacher of the Peoples Temple, appearing when he was a 21-year-old student pastor in Indianapolis. In Sunday school parable style, it described how a ragged tramp found himself near the Jones home at Lynn in the gathering dusk of an early Spring day.

"A young boy," the 1953 news account continued, "saw the lingering tramp and approached him. The ragged stranger would not raise his eyes as the boy questioned him about his home... Finally the tattered knight of the road muttered:

"'I don't have a friend in the world. I'm ready to give up.'

"The boy, barely through his first year of school,

looked at the tired, beaten old man and said firmly: 'What
do you mean, mister? God's your friend and I'm your
friend. And mom will help you get a job.' And 'Mom,'
Mrs. Lynetta Jones, did just that.

"That event of the rejuvenation of a man who had lost
hope marked a milestone in James Jones' life. His love of
humanity and his desire to help the unfortunate was
eventually to lead him to the ministry."

Shortly after the story appeared Jones opened a small
interdenominational church. He financed it by selling live
monkeys.

In 1949 he married Marceline Baldwin, a nurse. He
was at that time 18, just out of high school and not yet sure
whether he wanted to pursue a medical or clerical career.
Eventually they would have eight children, one natural
and seven by adoption of all races.

By the time Jones was thirty, with the first stirrings of
the national black "Movement," Jones was named
director of the Indianapolis Human Rights Commission.
His own reputation grew as he learned to manipulate the
strings of political, civic, and religious influence.
Laudatory stories continued in the press. He enlisted
blacks in his church, spoke out on civil rights matters, and
served free food to down-and-outers such as the tramp of
Lynn.

For two years, between 1961 and 1963, Jones struck
out on a new course. He left Indianapolis for Belo
Horizonte in Brazil where he worked as a missionary.
During his South American sojurn, he paid a brief visit to
Guyana. In Brazil he organized orphanages and a
mission. His own family emphasized the theme of
interracial harmony that was so dominant in his life.
Among his adopted children were a Korean and a black.
South America somehow must have exercised an allure
for Jones.

The church that he founded in 1953 was called the
Christian Assembly of God Church. Ten years later, he
changed the name to the Peoples Temple Full Gospel
Church. He was ordained in 1964 as a minister of the
Christian Church (Disciples of Christ), one of the main

line denominations with a membership of 1.3 million, mostly in the Midwest, with its headquarters in Indianapolis.

Jones also showed a penchant for entrepreneurial activity to go along with his ministerial work during the mid-1960s. He formed two nonprofit corporations in Indianapolis during 1965. One was called Wings of Deliverance and its stated purpose was "to further the Kingdom of God and spread the true holy word of God." The second corporation was called Jim-Lu-Mar Corp. and it was formed by Jones with his mother (Lynette) and his wife (Marceline). Its stated purpose was to acquire a broad range of enterprises from nursing homes to grocery stores.

Returning to the United States after his two years of evangelical work abroad, Jones became haunted by the first of his apocalyptic obsessions, the specter of nuclear holocaust. An article in *Esquire Magazine* published in 1966 convinced him that among the areas of the world most secure from a nuclear bomb attack and the ensuing radioactive fall-out were the Redwood Valley in northern California and, by coincidence, the thickly jungled Belo Horizonte region of Brazil.

In 1966 Jones led a procession of about 100 followers to the northern California town of Ukiah, some 100 miles north of San Francisco. There he purchased a church, simply named the Peoples Temple, and other property. From his Redwood Valley base, Jones spread his reputation and the church's influence to San Francisco and Los Angeles. His entire congregation would drive to the two cities on weekends to spread Jones's gospel and win adherents—and collect money. By the testimony of former members, such a weekend trip would pour $30,000 or more into Jones's church coffers.

Jones, early in his career, remarked to an acquaintance that he could have become a millionaire if he had not been called to God. "Everything I touch," he confided, "turns to money."

His financial successes were less accidental than Jones suggested. In fact, as former members would later testify, the Peoples Temple was a high-powered money machine systematically stripping its members of their earthly possessions and the public of fervently-hawked contributions. One former Temple member intimately acquainted with Jones's finances estimated that the church took in $65,000-a-month in Social Security checks.

Members such as the Mills signed over all their property to the Temple as gifts. "That's what made it so hard to leave," Mills said afterward. "We had nowhere to go and nothing to fall back on." Large sums of cash would shower into the collection plate during Temple services. Photographs of Reverend Jones would be sold to ward off burglars or rub on afflicted parts of the body. Life insurance policies were cashed to enhance the church treasury. Followers were expected at first to contribute a quarter of their salary to Jones, later 40 percent, and yet later virtually their entire earnings—taking back just enough for subsistence in Temple dormitories.

So bountiful was the shower of money into Jones's coffers that the Temple reportedly had 15 bank accounts and began transporting vast bundles of cash to the Guyana colony. As much as $50,000 would be sent by trusted couriers to the jungle mission. One former high official of the church claimed the Temple's books showed that at least $10 million had been stashed away in banks in Europe, Guyana, and California.

After the mass suicide, a cache estimated at hundreds of thousands of dollars in currency and checks was found with the cadavers of Jones and his followers.

In 1971 Jones made a major real estate move into metropolitan California by purchasing for $50,000 a buff-colored, block-shaped synagogue in San Francisco and a second church in Los Angeles. The purchase was paid off in several years. The opening services at the new Peoples Temple in Fillmore were dazzling, drawing crowds from all over the city. Soul and gospel singers, dance groups, speakers such as Angela Davis and American Indian leader Dennis Banks, together with faith-healing exhibitions, appealed to the musical, political, and medical tastes and yearnings of a large potential constituency. The

Peoples Temple became a showcase of social programs with its infirmary, child care center, carpentry shop, printing press, and kitchens, which fed hundreds daily.

The public benefactions of Jones and the Temple were richly chronicled in the press. They attracted national attention when *The New York Times* on September 11, 1976, carried a three column photograph and a story about a Peoples Temple picket line surrounding the Fresno County Courthouse to protest the jailing of four *Fresno Bee* newsmen on contempt of court charges. The *Times* article, by West Coast correspondent Wallace Turner, quoted Jones as saying:

"We feel that the Judeo-Christian tradition's most prominent concern is freedom. Where the spirit of God is, there's liberty. We've always been very freedom-conscious."

In a grateful editorial, the *Fresno Bee*, one of the influential McClatchy chain of newspapers, applauded the Temple for its supportive turn-out.

"It is difficult to watch the quiet demonstration of support for 'The *Bee* Four' in Courthouse Park without having tears of emotion cloud your vision," the *Bee* editorial said. "...This is what America is all about—defending each other's rights. Thank you, members of Peoples Temple, for showing it to others." A year later Jones and the California press would have far less complimentary things to say about each other.

In 1977 Jones ordered his minions on a protest march onto the Golden Gate Bridge, from which 600 persons have leaped to their death. They demanded the construction of an anti-suicide fence.

The *San Francisco Examiner* in January, 1976, carried a story headlined "Charity—Alive in the Tenderloin" describing the Peoples Temple's donation of $6000 to save an escort service provided for unprotected elderly persons in the city's Skid Row district. "I was so moved when I saw a photograph of a large young black man supporting a small white woman—in these times of alienation of the races," Jones was quoted as remarking as he handed over the check.

Most revealing of the press notices for Jones was a March, 1976, item by *San Francisco Chronicle* columnist Herb Caen—who is himself a West Coast journalistic institution—under the subheading PEOPLEWATCH.

"Ranged along the all-important East Wall of Bardelli's (a well-known San Francisco restaurant) a few noons ago: Ex-Mayor Elmer Robinson next to Ex-Mayor George Christopher next to Assemblyman Willie Brown next to the Reverend Jim Jones, head of the Peoples Temple . . . The Reverend Jones, head of an 8000-member church, is soft-spoken, modest, publicity-shy, and will not be pleased to see his name in the paper. Even well-intentioned publicity can be a detriment," he says apologetically. But, like Santa Claus, he knows when you've been good: many a San Franciscan and many a project have received sizable checks from the Peoples Temple, accompanied by only a short note from Jim Jones saying 'We appreciate what you are doing.'"

On November 21, 1978, after the grisly jungle suicide rites ordered by Jones, Caen wrote a sorrowful column. "I met Jim Jones twice," he wrote. "We had long lunches, early in his career here, before he became a political figure. I found him appealing—soft-spoken, modest, talking earnestly of helping people. If he was a con man, he was masterful at it . . . When I wrote a couple of favorable items about him, the mail flooded in from Peoples Temple members, almost every letter identical, as though they had been ordered. Unnerving . . ."

In 1973 a church expedition of 20 members travelled to Guyana to look for a site upon which to establish an agricultural mission for ghetto youths and others whose spirits could benefit from exposure to rural life. The following year Jones negotiated a lease with the Guyanese government for 27,000 acres in the heavily-jungled north near the town of Port Kaituma. The move was prompted by a fire in the San Francisco temple which heightened Jones's fears that there were sinister forces in the United States determined to extinguish the life of his church.

Jones attracted his stream of disciples from a wide front of social sectors: the survivors of the anti-war movement who had reached the end of the political ideologies of the 1960's; poor blacks—young and old—who found physical and emotional sustenance in the Temple; the elderly, who suffered pangs of loneliness and want; the religious, and political yearners for a better world, who saw the light in Jones's peculiar blend of apostolic socialism.

To understand the magnetism of Jones, it is necessary to see how he wove together with artful phrases his appeals to the humanitarian yearnings, the politics, and the physical vanities of his constituents.

Although his traditions were Christian fundamentalist, Jones held no conventional Christian notion of God. "Neither my colleagues nor I are any longer caught up in the opiate of religion..." he wrote in his church's magazine, *Peoples Forum*, in January, 1978. In a September, 1977, interview with *The New York Times* his wife of 28 years said that Jones was a Marxist who held that religion's trappings were useful only for social and economic uplift. "Jim has used religion to try to get some people out of the opiate of religion," she said. Once, in his wife's presence, Jones slammed down a Bible with the exclamation, "Marcie, I've got to destroy this paper idol."

In his own column, "Perspectives from Guyana," published in the church newspaper, Jones wrote lyrically of joys of pastoral life in Guyana and, at the same time, deplored the technological culture of the United States. However strange Jones's encomiums to life in the colony now sound in view of its terrible fate, the words must have described the psychic reality of a significant number of residents of Jonestown.

"The warm, gentle tradewinds have come up and the glow of evening is subsiding quickly into the clear, star-filled night," he wrote. "There is such peace here. There can't be anything so fulfilling anywhere as living this communal life...I work in the fields whenever I can—whenever I am not helping coordinate the defense against the attacks on us in the United States. It strikes me as immensely sad that the vast majority of people submit to the regimentation and extreme tension of a highly-

technological society. They pay such a high price in
strokes, hypertension, physical diseases, and mental
stress." The column went on to describe the caring,
communal, happy life in Guyana—"the high relationships here, ones that do not come just out of sex, but by
sharing and living the highest ideals. We have passed
beyond alienation and have found a way of living that
nurtures trust—one that could speak to a society grown
cynical and cold."

Of himself, Jones wrote "I know well that I am not as
articulate as Martin Luther King, Jr., Malcolm X, or
Eugene V. Debs, but my head is on straight and I am well-
trained for battle. No one could be more fearless or
principled."

To the religious, Jones offered religion; to the
ideological, he offered politics; to the ignorant and
gullible, he offered miracles. One such feat was the
"passing" of cancers, an illusion he managed to carry off
with bravura and ecstatic outcries from the audience. He
would pretend to extract a cancerous growth from the
throat or other parts of a victim, using chicken organs as
the prop. Sometimes a cooperating disciple would gag on
a gizzard or liver that Jones had jammed down the hapless
member's throat to induce the cancer's "passing." It made
for greater realism.

Such acts of chicanery, together with the increasing
brutalization of the Temple rites, plus Jones's ever more
bizarre behavior drove one after another of the faithful
into first withdrawal from, then active opposition to the
Temple and its leader. Mills and others formed a deprogramming center for the cult victims they called the
Human Freedom Center ("Dedicated to helping people
assume personal responsibility for their own lives").

Hundreds of others would remain within the increasingly isolated confines of the Peoples Temple and would
follow the Reverend Jim Jones into the jungle to the
communal destruction against which he warned them and
for which, in one of the church's most ominous rites, he
had also prepared them.

5.

The Jungle Utopia

Our twin engine Havilland, chartered from Guyana Airways and piloted by Guy Spence, was airborne from Georgetown's Timehri airport at 2:30 P.M. on Friday, November 17.

The passenger list included Congressman Leo J. Ryan, his aide, Jackie Speier; Mark Lane and Charles E. Garry, Jonestown's two lawyers; Richard Dwyer, the deputy chief of mission at the U.S. Embassy in Georgetown; nine newsmen, including myself; Neville Annibourne, the friendly if somewhat bumbling Guyanese government information officer who was still trying to determine if this "investigation" was somehow going to embarrass his country; and four of the Concerned Relatives who had come all the way from California, hoping to persuade their loved ones to leave Jonestown, which the relatives were now certain was a jungle Gulag.

By nightfall the next day, some of these people would be dead. Others would be badly wounded. But as we took off, my own feeling was one of satisfaction that I had gotten aboard.

The competition for seats on the plane had been keen. The party of Concerned Relatives who had arrived in Georgetown with Ryan numbered 17. There wasn't room for all of them on the plane. They reluctantly agreed to send only four people from their group and give the rest of the available seats to the news people. They thought it was important for the journalists to get into the Peoples Temple Agricultural Project at Jonestown and tell the world what they found.

The journalists put a lot of pressure on Ryan for seats, too. We represented *The Washington Post,* NBC, the *San Francisco Chronicle,* the *San Francisco Examiner,* and a private news agency in Los Angeles run by Gordon Lindsay, who had first suggested this story to my newspaper and had offered to cover it for us. We made it clear to Ryan that we and our news organizations would be very unhappy if any of us were bumped from this flight. Earlier in the day we had talked among ourselves about giving Ryan an "all or none" edict. But that wouldn't have worked, in any case, because each of us wanted the story first-hand and would have insisted on being aboard. The problem was solved by the Concerned Relatives, who agreed that all of us should go. Those left behind had high hopes that they would get into Jonestown on another flight the next day. But none of us had any inkling of what the next 24 hours were to bring.

On the hour's flight to Port Kaituma, the airstrip near Jonestown, I sat next to Mark Lane, who had made a career out of challenging official theories about the assassinations of John Kennedy and Martin Luther King, Jr. He believed in conspiracies.

My first interest in him was to convince him that if any newsman got into Jonestown on this mission, it ought to be me. We were still uncertain what would happen when we landed and had been given no assurance that anyone would get to the Peoples Temple except Ryan, Speier, and the man from the Embassy, Dwyer.

I found Lane interesting. Contrary to what I had heard and read about him, he seemed to be a reasonable and intelligent man. Beyond that, he seemed more open-minded about Jones and Jonestown than I had expected. He was full of praise for "Father" and his socialist commune. But he admitted that there were probably people there who wanted to leave. His guess was that maybe 10 percent of the residents would get out if they had a chance, although he insisted that nothing more than "peer pressure" was being used to keep them in the jungle settlement.

He told me he was not an "authority" on Jonestown, but said he had visited the place a month before and had been extremely impressed. He called it a truly socialist community, interracial, and genuinely religious in its own way: "A most incredible society in the middle of the jungle."

Lane was particularly impressed with Jonestown's medical staff, which the next day would prepare the cyanide potion that killed more than 900 Jonestown residents. "I had the best physical exam (at Jonestown) I've had anywhere," he told me. He said it was given the previous month.

As we prepared to land, he said, "I believe that 90 percent of the people there will fight to the death to remain. I think it's really true. They know what they're doing is not in the mainstream of American society and they feel that the (U.S.) government is coming after them again. Now, I'm not saying they're right, but that's how they feel."

During the flight, Lane asked me what I thought about the Peoples Temple and Jonestown. I told him, quite truthfully, that I had never heard of it before my editors called me in Caracas and told me to join Ryan in Georgetown, that I had decided not to file any stories based on the allegations of the Concerned Relatives because the charges seemed absolutely outrageous, that I wanted very much to see the community for myself, and that I was coming into this with an open mind.

But I also told Lane that if I was denied admission,
I would be left with little more than the charges and
whatever Ryan had to say and that my editors were
expecting a story. It would be the Peoples Temple's
fault if, by denying me access, the result was largely
negative. Lane, who, if nothing else, understands the
press, said he hoped to get at least some of the
journalists aboard into Jonestown: "I have been
insisting, from the first day I met them, to let
everybody in."

But he was still protective of Jones and Jonestown. Our pilot overflew the jungle commune on our
way in for the landing. Lane and Garry objected
loudly. They said an earlier overflight had caused an
elderly woman to suffer a heart attack. But they
neglected to tell us that the cause of the heart attack
may have been Jones's irrational warnings to his
flock that an invasion of the settlement was
imminent and that the CIA, FBI, and other U.S.
agencies intended to destroy Jonestown. Our
overflight, Lane and Garry insisted, could only
create fear and hostility in Jonestown and complicate our mission.

Pilot Spence put the twin Otter aircraft down on
the Port Kaituma strip. The time, according to the
flight log, was 3:41 P.M. We were five miles from the
Jonestown settlement.

Waiting for us at the side of the crude runway
were the Jonestown dump truck and tractor, several
representatives of the commune, and the local
constabulary, headed by Corporal Umil Rudder, a
short, lean black man who had neither identification
nor uniform. But his second-in-command had a gun,
so there was no point in arguing very much when the
Peoples Temple representatives told us that Ryan,
Speier, Lane, Garry, and Dwyer would proceed
immediately to Jonestown while the rest of us would
wait near the plane—under guard.

"I was informed by my superior in Georgetown
that Peoples Temple do not request parties present

into the Peoples Temple," Rudder told us in his Guyanan patois after the dump truck and tractor pulled out with Ryan and the others. We had heard that Jim Jones and the Guyanese government worked hand-in-glove, that Jones could do pretty much what he wanted within Guyana and that Ptolemy Reid, the country's Deputy Prime Minister, was a particularly close and influential friend of the Bishop's.

Whether the closeness was due to Jonestown's socialist principles and its success in opening jungle areas that previously had been sparsely populated and unproductive agriculturally—or whether, as the relatives claimed, it was because Jones gave large sums of money and provided attractive young women to Guyanese government officials—we couldn't know.

But Corporal Rudder's presence at the airstrip and his refusal to let us leave the immediate vicinity of the plane, even though we had a letter from the Home Affairs Ministry saying that we didn't need permission to visit this part of Guyana—a negative way of saying we had permission—only confirmed that, whatever the reasons, Jonestown had a lot of influence in its adopted land.

As we milled around, sweating in the late afternoon heat, the guard with the gun, whose name I never did get, became somewhat friendly. He told us that every now and then, once or twice a month, private planes would land at the airstrip and pick up badly injured Americans from Jonestown. The guard told us that the townspeople and police were always told that the Americans had been injured while working with machetes or machinery, but the guard made it clear that he thought the "accidents" that seemed to occur so frequently were more than a little suspicious.

"When you go there, keep your eyes open," he said to me. "We really hate those people. Reverend Jones should have died a long time ago." I duly noted in my notebook what the guard had told me. It was 5:30 P.M. "Guard begins to open up," I jotted down next to what he had to say.

I still wasn't convinced Jonestown was evil; it was, after all, possible that hundreds of Americans, transported from cities in the United States to this godforsaken jungle, might not know very much about farm machinery. It didn't even surprise me that the locals might not like the foreigners in their midst.

But I kept the guard's words in the back of my mind. I was surprised at this antagonism by the Guyanese in Port Kaituma toward the Americans at Jonestown. I was determined to "keep my eyes open" if I ever got a chance to see the place that I was hearing so much about.

At exactly 6 P.M., the tractor from Jonestown returned to the airstrip. The woman driver announced that we would all be allowed to enter the commune—all except Gordon Lindsay, who would have to return to Georgetown on the plane. Immediately. Lindsay, who had written a long expose of the Peoples Temple that the *National Inquirer* had not published but which the Temple, we would later learn, somehow got a copy of, was persona non grata. At the time, he was undoubtedly terribly disappointed that he would not see the place he had spent so much time researching and writing about. Of course, that unpublished article probably saved his life.

At 6:16 P.M., the Guyana Airways plane, piloted by Spence and with only Lindsay aboard, took off from Port Kaituma for the hour's flight back to Georgetown. I noted in my notebook "we have no idea of how we get out" since the plane had been chartered only for one round trip and there had been no arrangements for it to return the next day.

It was obvious we were going to spend the night, although we didn't know exactly where. But I figured the embassy back in Georgetown would get us out somehow—after all, leaving a Congressman stranded in the jungle would never do, no matter how much the State Department might like Congress to be abolished so that the "dips" could run U.S. foreign policy all by themselves.

At 6:19 P.M., the Jonestown dump truck arrived to fetch us from the airstrip. We piled aboard—tired, hot, and sweaty. It took almost an hour-and-a-half for the truck to fight its way through the oozing mud which serves as the one and only road between Port Kaituma and Jonestown. It was pitch black as we rounded the last curve and saw the commune, its electric lights blazing in the distance. I kept thinking that it looked like a scene out of *Gone with the Wind*, not because the buildings were the same but because, as we drew closer, old black women were baking bread in the bakery, people were washing clothes in the laundry, black and white children were chasing each other in the little park, and long lines of people, mostly black, were waiting for their suppers.

It seemed so peaceful, so orderly, so bucolic. There to greet us as we got off the dump truck was the white Mizzuz, Marceline Jones, surrounded, at a discreet distance, but obviously adoring—or scared—young people, ready to run an errand or carry a message. Marcie, as Mrs. Jones was called, greeted us warmly and informed us that our supper was ready up at the central open air pavilion where her husband, the man we had heard so much about, was waiting to meet us.

I noted immediately that, contrary to what the Concerned Relatives had told us, nobody seemed to be starving. Indeed, everyone seemed quite healthy. I began to walk, alone, up toward the main building at the center of Jonestown, thinking that, considering everything, this little place was rather pleasant. I could see how someone might want to live here.

As I was walking, a guy who looked about 26 or 27 introduced himself as Tim Carter and fell in alongside me. He asked my name and when I told him, he smiled. "Mark Lane told us about you. He

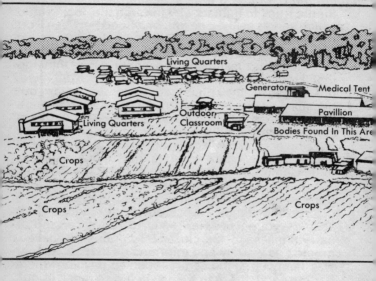

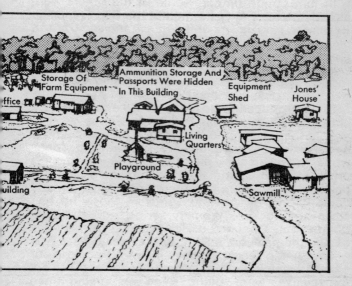

said the reporter from *The Post* seemed sensitive
and fair. It's good to have you here." As we reached
the pavilion, I saw there was a big table in the center,
large enough to seat 30 or more people. Carter went
around to one side and asked me if I wanted to sit
with him during dinner. Some of the others were
already there: Tim Reiterman of the *San Francisco
Examiner;* Ron Javers of the *San Francisco Chronicle,* Greg Robinson, the *Examiner* photographer;
Don Harris of NBC. Mark Lane and Charles E. Garry
were seated across the table talking to a man in his
forties, who wore a red sports shirt, and glasses and
had jet black hair. He sat at the head of the table.
Carter introduced me to him and he leaned across to
shake my hand. He was Father Jim Jones.

I sat there talking to Carter for a moment. Javers
and Reiterman were already interviewing Jones
while Robinson took pictures. Don Harris and his
crew were unloading their equipment beside the
pavilion, near where Leo Ryan was sitting, already
talking, one by one, to some of those he had
requested to see. Women served coffee before
dinner. The Concerned Relatives sat on benches
beside the pavilion, talking to their relatives.

Everything seemed to be going well. People in our
party were doing exactly what they had come to do:
the relatives were talking, Ryan was talking, Lane
and Garry were counseling, and the newsmen were
interviewing. Considering all of the problems we had
had getting here, the Jonestown people seemed
quite hospitable. I couldn't understand why there
had been such a fuss; the buildings were impressive,
the people seemed healthy, rational, and friendly. If
any of the awful things we had been told were true,
they weren't apparent. I was, on the whole, impressed.

As plastic trays with hot pork sandwiches, greens,
and potato-like roots were served, more and more
Jonestown people quietly took seats in the pavilion.
The lights dimmed and the Jonestown band,

accompanying a singer, began to play, first the Guyanese national anthem and then "America the Beautiful." The music and the singers were good enough to be professional. The show had begun.

I finished my dinner and decided to walk over to where Ryan was sitting, smoking a cigarette. It didn't seem appropriate to smoke at the table, Jonestown residents, we had been told, did not smoke or drink alcohol.

Ryan motioned me over. I asked him how things were going and if he had learned anything to confirm his suspicions. He said no, not really. But then he pointed out a white man, who was dressed in overalls, about 45, tall, with a graying crewcut.

The man seemed almost in a trance as he clapped to the soul music that filled the pavilion. Ryan pointed out that all the people—maybe 700 in all—were, like this man, standing and clapping along with the music. Strange, wasn't it, Ryan said. The teenagers might get off on soul music but middle-aged men and 70-year-old women? It was an observation I wouldn't forget.

Ryan was very impressed by the scene. As the music poured out, people from the Temple came up for interviews with the Congressman and, after a while he stood up, took the microphone, and declared:

"I can tell you right now that by the few conversations I've had with some of the folks here already this evening that...there are some people who believe this is the best thing that ever happened in their whole lives."

The crowd cheered for nearly twenty minutes.

I left Ryan and wandered to the other side of the pavilion, where groups of young people, black and white, were sitting on or leaning against a guard rail, listening to the music, talking among themselves. They weren't clapping so intently and seemed far more natural. But as I approached they kind of faded away, regrouping a short distance off.

But then, always, someone would come up to me and say "hi." They would ask where I was going and ask if I was interested in the music. I said yes, but I could hear it from where I was. I was interested in seeing some of the Jonestown buildings nearby, which seemed so sturdy, clean, and well-designed.

Each time, I was told that there were probably people asleep in the cabins. But I shouldn't worry, there would be a tour the next morning and I would see everything I wanted. I didn't feel I could just enter a building on my own—that would be intruding in a way I thought might be improper—and I could tell that no one was going to invite me inside. I decided to go back to the pavilion and listen to Jones, who was talking to the other reporters, flanked by his lawyers and several young, mostly white, people I would later learn were his top lieutenants.

As the conversation proceeded, the show went on—loud music, singing, rhythmic clapping. Jones rambled as he talked. Theme after theme crept into the dialogue. His mood changed, depending on the subject. He had told us that he might have cancer, that he had lost 31 pounds in recent months, that his temperature had reached 103 degrees that day, and that "in many ways I feel like I'm dying. I've never felt like this before. Who the hell knows what stress can do to you."

He was asked about Tim and Grace Stoen and their conflicting claims about six-year-old John-John. "I can't give her the child," he responded. "Oh, God, it's so painful, it's so painful. I feel so guilty about it."

He said that he, not Tim Stoen, was the father of the child: "He's my son. He's my son."

I asked him then if it would be correct to say that he had had an affair with Grace. He said: "I never had an affair with anyone but my wife." But he also said that Tim Stoen had asked him to have sexual relations with Grace. "I needed him (Stoen) in the church at that time," Jones said. "He asked me to do it and I did it." This relationship with Grace, Jones said, continued for four years.

"I stayed with her until she asked me to marry her," he said. "She's a manipulative, seductive female. I would not like to hurt her, but I know whose child it is . . . I can't give her the child. Oh, God, it's so painful, it's so painful. I feel so guilty about it."

But at another point he said, "I would give him John Jones (John-John) if John wanted to go." He claimed that the boy was happy in Jonestown and that Grace and Tim Stoen had willingly left the child in his care several years before.

I sat beside him and watched him closely as he talked. Grace Stoen had told me that he used an eyebrow pencil to give an appearance of thickness to his sideburns. I was curious about that and, after looking at him for a while, decided she was right.

I had heard during my time with the relatives in Georgetown a great deal about sex between Jones and people in the Temple. I had also heard that at various times Jones had ordered his followers not to have sex with each other, even husbands and wives. After he admitted to us his affair with Grace Stoen and that he had fathered John-John, I asked him if people in Jonestown were allowed to have normal sexual lives.

One of his lieutenants, seated next to me, was named Sarah Tropp. She answered my question: "Bullshit. All I have to say is bullshit. People do fuck in Jonestown."

Jones then said people in the church were required to take counseling before marriage. But he said 30 babies had been born in the commune since the summer of 1977. There was no more conversation with him that night about sex.

But he was voluble on other subjects. It became clear, for example, that he viewed anyone who criticized or defected from the Temple as part of a conspiracy, aimed at destroying him and his movement. "Threat, threat, threat of extinction," he thundered. "I wish I wasn't born at times. I understand hate; love and hate are very close. They can have me."

I was still trying to get an understanding of what this movement was about. Was it political or religious, Christian or Communist? He claimed it was all of these, which left me more confused.

At one point, he said he was a Marxist. But when I asked if this was a religious movement, he said: "Yes, very much."

Still later after he had talked about his belief in the value of "living together, working together, sharing work, goods, and services," I asked if it was correct to describe him as a socialist. That upset him. "Call me a socialist, I've been called worse," he said, and then launched into a long tirade.

"I do not believe in violence," he said in an agitated voice. "Violence corrupts. And then they say I want power. What kind of power do I have walking down the path talking to my little old seniors (elderly residents). I hate power. I hate money. The only thing I wish now is that I was never born. All I want is peace. I'm not worried about my image. If we could just stop it. But if we don't I don't know what's going to happent to 1,200 lives here."

Through all this, his lawyers, Garry and Lane, had little to say. He would turn to them now and then when the questions touched on various legal issues or lawsuits involving the Temple.

After his denunciation of violence, power, and money, the music show in the pavilion stopped. The lights were turned on and Jones, obviously tired and ill, asked if our lodgings had been arranged. One of his aides assured him that the reporters and relatives in our party had arranged to spend the night at Port Kaituma, that there was a dance we wanted to go to in town.

I was infuriated. No arrangements of any kind had been made. I told Jones that he had no obligation to put us up for the night, but it simply wasn't true that we had a place to sleep. Marceline, his wife, whispered to him within earshot of me that she could arrange to find another 10 or 15 beds without too much difficulty. He told her angrily, "It's a mistake, it's a mistake. I don't want them here. Someone will have to arrange something in Port Kaituma."

It bothered me that, after an earlier display of ostentatious hospitality, Jones was now sending us out in the dump truck in the middle of the night. But I said nothing more to him.

Before leaving Jonestown that night, I had another conversation with Sarah Tropp and her brother, Richard, headmaster of the high school at the settlement.

They impressed me as intelligent, articulate, and well-educated people. They were able to explain to me in a far more lucid way than Jones the reasons people had come to this settlement in the jungle of Guyana. Many of the older and poorer blacks, they said, had gladly traded their lives in the city ghettoes of the United States for the society here, where there was no crime, no deprivation, and where people "cared for each other." As for themselves, the Tropps were prototypes of American intellectuals who had gone through the civil rights and anti-war turmoil of the '60s and '70s and were now seeking the good society they had never found at home. They were dedicated socialists with a very clear idea of what the good society meant to them. It meant Jonestown.

We became friendly during this brief encounter. They sensed that something was bothering me. My question was: if Jim Jones is so open and caring about people and if Jonestown has nothing to hide, why couldn't we spend the night there? Why were we being ordered off to Port Kaituma?

I told them I had heard Marceline Jones tell her husband that she could find room for us here, but that he angrily told her that he wanted us out.

The Tropps had nothing to say. I told them good-night and followed the others down to the dump truck. Just as I was climbing aboard, someone ran up to me and said Mark Lane wanted to see me before I left. Lane and Sarah Tropp appeared and told me that if I wanted to stay, I was welcome, but that the others would have to go on. I decided that if I got special treatment it would cause more trouble with the other reporters than it was worth. I thanked them and got on the truck.

After a bumpy and slow return trip to Port Kaituma we were taken to the Weekend Discotheque, where the owner, a man named Mike, had been persuaded by someone in Jonestown to let us sleep on the floor that night. It was then 11:30 P.M. The discotheque was empty except for our party.

We sat around drinking beer and rum, smoking cigarettes, and hashing over our initial impressions of Jonestown. Anthony Katsaris, one of the Concerned Relatives, had a sister, Maria, in the settlement. It seemed to be generally known that Maria was the current mistress of Jim Jones. I asked him about his meeting with her. He said she was distant and that she had given no indication that she wanted to leave Jonestown.

Within an hour or so, a Guyanese guard from the airstrip showed up, obviously wanting to talk about Jonestown.

He had a few beers with us and asked us to walk to his police station with him where he had things to tell us. Javers, Reiterman, and I went with him. At the station, he told us that he knew there was at least one automatic rifle at Jonestown that had been registered and approved by the Guyanese government. Furthermore, he confirmed details of the escape of one Jonestown man who had managed to get back to San Francisco, where he had been interviewed previously by Reiterman. This escapee had told Reiterman he had been beaten at Jonestown, but had no scars to prove it. The guard confirmed the man's story and said he had been badly beaten before his escape.

It was now 3 A.M. We headed back to the Weekend Discotheque to go to sleep. At the end of this long, exhausting day, I was still skeptical of most of the allegations I had heard against Jones and Jonestown. I was convinced that Jones was a very sick man and might be mentally unbalanced. But the settlement itself had left a favorable impression in my mind, as had several of the Temple members who had talked to me, especially the Tropps. I wasn't ready to conclude that Jonestown was a jungle Gulag.

I went to sleep on the floor. So did Harris, NBC cameraman Bob Brown, and photographer Greg Robinson of the *San Francisco Examiner.* It was to be their last night on earth. In the morning we would return to Jonestown.

6.

THE PEOPLES TEMPLE:
Handwriting on the Wall

At the end of July, 1977, the magazine *New West* shook the Temple to its foundations with a detailed investigative article that also hit San Francisco like a bombshell. Even before the article by *San Francisco Chronicle* reporter Marshall Kilduff and *New West*'s Phil Tracy, the magazine was under siege by letter and telephone threat from friends of the Peoples Temple. Lieutenant Governor Dymally called Frank Lalli, the magazine's managing editor, to counsel against publishing an unfavorable article on Jones and his church. A letter writer warned that the magazine had failed to realize "the precarious faith people from disadvantaged background have and their proclivity toward militant reaction to what they perceive as an unfair or unwarranted attack."

Said a *New West* editor: "I'm not ready to label that a threat, but I have to admit I feel threatened." The *San Francisco Chronicle* reported: "The atmosphere at *New West* magazine these days resembles a military encampment under siege."

When the article did make its appearance, it chronicled for the first time publicly the beatings, the extortions, and

the humiliating rites of the Peoples Temple—all in the
words of former members who had until then been too
afraid to speak out.

The text of that article could have been, in a metaphor
from the Bible, the handwriting on the wall for the
Temple of Jim Jones. It started the tremors of public
doubt, emboldened those who knew to talk, and sealed
with permanence the flight of Reverend Jones to the site
in Guyana which had been consecrated with his name and
was now his place of final exile.

The *New West* story pulled the plug on a sudden
torrent of revelations to come in the press. It helped to
generate a series of civil suits against Jones and the church
filed by former members who claimed to have been
defrauded not only of money but fleeced of their own
children and other loved ones. The truth that began to
emerge was that, behind his glowing public facade, Jones
had managed to conceal a private nightmare world which
he ruled. In that world Jones, as "Father", imposed a
regimen of terror, physical punishment, exhaustion,
emotional dependency, and communal tyranny on his
followers.

It was a paradoxical world in which Jones enticed his
disciples with the charisma of his personality and then
reduced them to what would have to be described, by any
objective measure, as a state of abject religious serfdom.
Poverty, grinding labor, fear, and punishment were the
staples of Jim Jones's utopian colony—and eventual mass
suicide.

To understand the paradox it is necessary to hear some
of the testimony of those who broke away from the
hypnotic influence of Jones and also to look at some
common denominators of cult behavior both today and
in history.

Al and Jeanie Mills joined the Temple in Ukiah at the
end of 1969, eventually taking five of their children with
them. Six years later they left the church, stripped of their
property by the Temple and with memories of lives of
unrelieved anguish. Mills and his wife are intelligent,
educated citizens. When they joined the church their
names were Elmer and Deanna Mertle. They changed

their name legally to Mills after fleeing Jones because of documents they claimed they had signed under duress when their lives were under the control of the Temple. Their case was first briefly described in the *New West* article and then the couple filed a $1.1 million lawsuit against Jones, charging that they had been beaten, then cheated of their property. They charged Jones with fraud, false imprisonment, and misrepresentation.

"We went into the group thinking it was a very warm, loving family," Al Mills remembered. "It was a beautiful and cohesive group. I was always involved in civil rights activity myself. I helped blacks exert themselves in politics." He had been chairman of the Contra Costa, California, County Council of Churches Social Action Committee.

Mills was impressed with Jones's commitment to "progressive politics," though he was initially repelled by the pastor's claims of faith-healing powers. "When people would start telling us about the healings, I told my wife, 'Jesus, what the hell are we getting into?'"

But eventually even Mills found himself giving some credence to the claimed miracles. "Jones," he said, "was so charismatic that he could talk at one meeting to very religious people about healings and at another to very political people about justice. You heard what you wanted to hear. I knew that some of the healings were phony and staged.

"But if that's the level people are at and it gets them to work for social justice, then that's fine."

As time passed, the early political idyll of life in the colony turned gradually into a nightmare from which they barely managed to extricate themselves. Speaking of Jones and his techniques of control, Mills said, "His strategy was to divide and conquer. He'd use Hitler's tactic—using children to tattle on their parents. It was so effective in breaking up marriages.

"You couldn't talk to your wife. Fortunately, my wife and I had made a pact that we would never stop talking to one another and we would never stop having sex with one another."

Jones was described by Mills as a "genius" at stripping

away the egos of his parishioners at all-night "catharsis" sessions during which they would be denounced, beaten, and humiliated by Jones and the rest of the congregation. "The beatings started gradually and, in meetings where beatings were taking place, if anyone expressed displeasure, they would be called forth and beaten themselves."

The Temple had its own brand of political theater. A favorite theme was the lynching of blacks by the Ku Klux Klan of which Jones had his own childhood memories.

Diana Mills, 18, is the daughter of Al and Jeanie. She, too, has anguishing memories of life in the Peoples Temple, where she spent her full adolescence. For her, things started to sour in the colony in 1972. That was when she remembered the beatings beginning—beatings which were getting "brutal and just sick." She watched her own sister, Linda, being beaten 75 times with a board until her buttocks were black, a beating so severe that the Mills girl was unable to sit for a week-and-a-half. "They held a microphone to her mouth," Diana recalled, "so everyone could hear her screams."

The punishment was exacted because Linda was seen in a parking lot hugging a girlfriend who had left the church. Jones charged that the Mills daughter had consorted with a lesbian.

Sex played a major role in Jones's governing of the Temple's flock. It was another manipulative lever by which he could control totally the lives under his command—rewarding or punishing and, to a considerable degree, seek his own gratification.

The testimony of former members of the colony after his death was that Jones used sex to dominate and blackmail members, having his secretary arrange his own sexual liaisons with men as well as women. Al Mills, once the Temple's membership chairman, stated, "She would call up and say, 'Father hates to do this, but he has this tremendous urge and could you please...'"

At the same time he would order gruesome public punishments for homosexual offenses. On one occasion, he exhorted his followers to continue beating a man accused of homosexual activity who had already been beaten to a pulp. "Kick him where he deserves it," the Pastor of the Peoples Temple was quoted as having shouted.

Mike Cartmell, a former associate minister of Jones's, said that Jones tried to make himself the "only legitimate object of sexual desire in the Temple." He remembers Jones claiming that he would engage in six-hour bouts of sexual activity boasting that it "totally obliterates" the personalities of his partners.

On December 12, 1973, Jones was arrested in a Hollywood theater for lewd conduct on the testimony of a Los Angeles police undercoverman to whom Jones had tried to make sexual advances. The charge was subsequently dismissed in a dispute over the legality of the arrest.

There were other corroborating accounts than those of the Mills's. *New West* recounted the case of Grace and Tim Stoen, who had been drawn to the Temple by the humanitarian notes of the Jones gospel and who rose to high position in the church hierarchy. Grace Stoen, by whom Jones claimed to have fathered the son, John-John, was the first to become disenchanted at the ritual brutalities and financial practices of Jones. She broke away in July, 1976, and began a custody action to regain possession of her son. Her husband followed her a year later and both were in Georgetown on the fearful morning when word came of the mass suicides in Jonestown—and the death their boy probably never had a choice about. Jones kept the Stoen child in his own household at the colony. So visibly attached to the boy was Jones that some followers believed the possible loss of John may have been central in the preacher's decision to go ahead with the flight to Guyana and, later, the suicides. It is doubtful, however, that any competent witness on that point survived the holocaust.

"The story of Jim Jones and his Peoples Temple is not over," the *New West* article predicted. "In fact, it has only begun to be told." How right the magazine was.

Deborah Layton Blakey was 18, a pretty girl from a well-to-do Berkeley family fresh out of a British boarding

school, when she joined the Peoples Temple. Her parents
had sent her to England to get away from the cult-ridden
scene on the West Coast. There, ironically, she met and
married a young Englishman of fundamentalist Christian
views who had heard of the Peoples Temple and they
joined. "I had grown up in affluent circumstances in the
permissive atmosphere of Berkeley, California," she said
in a June 15, 1978, affidavit describing publicly for the
first time conditions in Jonestown. "By joining the
Peoples Temple, I hoped to help others and, in the
process, to bring structure and self-discipline to my own
life."

Blakey, although not among the first batch of former
Peoples Temple members willing to tell their story to *New
West*, was in fact among the most important whistle-
blowers of the cult. Her affidavit (see Appendix D)
detailed the gruesome conditions in the Guyana colony in
detailed and prophetic terms which will be described
later. She also analyzed the sinister changes in the
personality and ruling style of Jones.

"During the years I was a member of the Peoples
Temple," Blakey attested, "I watched the organization
depart with increasing frequency from its professed
dedication to social change and participatory democracy.
The Reverend Jones gradually assumed a tyrannical hold
over the lives of Temple members.

"Any disagreement with his dictates came to be
regarded as 'treason.' The Reverend Jones labelled any
person who left the organization a 'traitor' and 'fair
game.' He steadfastly and convincingly maintained that
the punishment for defection was death. The fact that
severe corporal punishment was frequently administered
to Temple members gave the threats a frightening air of
reality.

"The Reverend Jones," Blakey went on, "saw himself
as the center of a conspiracy. The identity of the
conspirators changed from day to day along with his
erratic world vision. He induced the fear in others that,
through their contact with him, they had become targets
of the conspiracy.

"He convinced black Temple members that, if they did not follow him to Guyana, they would be put into concentration camps and killed. White members were instilled with the belief that their names appeared on a secret list of enemies of the state that was kept by the CIA and they would be tracked down, tortured, imprisoned, and subsequently killed if they did not flee to Guyana."

To reinforce his own authority over the flock and to also give voice to his own paranoid visions of a world outside ruled by malign, dark forces, Reverend Jones would rant for hours at a time—often all night—at his congregation. He would claim, on occasions, that he was the reincarnation of Lenin or Christ or Buddha, that he had divine powers to heal the sick, that he had powerful connections with the Mafia, with Idi Amin, or the Soviet government.

"When I first joined the Temple," Blakey related, "Reverend Jones seemed to make clear distinctions between fantasy and reality. I believed that most of the time when he said irrational things, he was aware that they were irrational, but that they served as a tool of his leadership. His theory was that the end justified the means.

"At other times, she wrote, "he appeared to be deluded by a paranoid vision of the world. He would not sleep for days at a time and talked compulsively about the conspiracies against him. However, as time went on, he appeared to become genuinely irrational."

Blakey believed that the final crisis of Jones and the church was triggered by Grace and Tim Stoen's apostasy and their effort to regain custody of their six-year-old son. The departure from the Temple of Grace Stoen, who had served as Chief Counselor of the church and was popular with the membership, was in itself a threat to Jones's control. Tim had been one of his most trusted advisors and, as Blakey put it, an adverse public statement by Timothy Stoen "would increase the tarnish" on Jones's image.

So frantic had Jones become over the Stoens' custody battle for their son that one morning in September 1977 a hysterical radio message came to the Temple in San Francisco from Jones in Guyana. Blakey was ordered to place telephone calls to high-ranking Guyanese officials who were visiting the United States and deliver this threat:

"Unless the government of Guyana takes immediate steps to stall the Guyanese court action regarding John Stoen's custody, the entire population of Jonestown would extinguish itself in a mass suicide by 5:30 P.M. that day."

Just a few hours later, the suicide threat was withdrawn, at least for the time being.

Mass suicide was one of the recurring themes in the frenzied dramatic ritualism of the Peoples Temple. Other witnesses had attested to the occasions when Jones gathered the congregation about him, including the children, and invited them to drink of a sacramental liquid in a weird parody of the communion rite. After all had partaken, Jones would announce that they had drunk poison.

Wanda Johnson, a 42-year-old former disciple whose son, Tommy Kice, was to die in the cult's endgame in Guyana, described the eerie experience:

"We were all given wine and if we didn't like it Jones said drink it anyway. They collected the cups and Jones informed us we had just drunk poison and would be dead within 30 minutes.

"Some people psychologically thought they were dying and fell off their chairs. I felt worried about my baby in Guyana. Jones assured us that they all had been taken care of—killed—and we were all who were left.

"Across from me, Andy Silvers, one of the few members of the Planning Commission of the church who knew, jumped up and said 'You mean we're all going to die?' and another member began beating him. Andy fell to the ground and a vial of phony blood spilled onto the floor. That's when I knew that something wasn't right.

"One woman ran to die with her baby and she was shot in the side. I thought it was real, but it was a blank. She dropped on the floor. There was a hole in her dress, just to give it reality.

"After Jones watched our torment in agony for the required time," said Wanda Johnson, "he told us it was just a test of our loyalty to him.

"We all knew he was mad, but we were compromised to the point that we could not question him."

Terror was one method by which Jones reinforced his authority over his subjects. To some degree, the suicide ritual was the ultimate demonstration of his power over his disciples and their dependency upon him. Power and dependency were two of the most primal bonds in the emotional structure of the Peoples Temple.

It was Rabbi Maurice Davis, who had sold a synagogue in Indianapolis to Jones for his Temple who later mused, after learning of the ritualistic suicide in Guyana: "I keep thinking what happens when the power of love is twisted into the love of power."

Jones's personal charisma was immediately apparent to a newcomer to his Temple.

"It's hard to describe the attraction," said Tom Dickson, a 53-year-old former follower, "But he had a way of convincing people he was something he wasn't. He was pleasant, well-spoken, appealing. He was dynamic in voice and gesture and imposing in appearance. He knew when to shout or lower his voice."

At the same time, said Dickson, once he had committed a follower to his flock, he took possession of the new member. "He was making slaves out of them. They were mostly young people, lower class people and women. He had them painting his house, fixing his car. I can look back now and understand how other things happened . . . the Manson slayings . . ."

But there was another tool of control. It was blackmail. Sexual, financial, political, or otherwise.

"When we went to a city, Reverend Jones's inner core group—his angels or assassination group—would photograph or tape record people sexually," said Wanda Johnson. This technique, she said, would be used to blackmail officials.

"I wrote letters that I hated my sons, that I had sexually molested them when they were infants, and that I would kill them if necessary because I hated them. Who would believe me if they saw these letters?" she added.

The church was built on a four-tiered structure of authority. The innermost group was called the angels; next came the planning commission, and then the security force—Jones's armed militia. At the top of the pyramid was, of course, the founder himself.

Teresa Cobb, a comely 26-year-old black woman who was brought into the church by her parents in 1966 and quit on her own initiative in 1972, described Jones's manipulation of sex and humiliation to enforce discipline in the Temple:

"One guy in the planning commission had fallen asleep during a long lecture—Jones would sometimes lecture and lecture. They tried to wake him up, but he would not. The man, Steve Addison, a white, was told to do a perverted sex act with a woman as punishment. He got sick and was beaten. He suffered a concussion and his nose was swollen to twice its normal size.

"Al Mills took a picture of him and gave it to Jones. Jones showed the picture of Addison to the congregation and said, "You think you got it bad. Look at what the planning commission has to go through."

Teresa Cobb's mother had first joined Jones's congregation in Indiana and moved westward with the minister. "In Indiana, we had it up to the yin yang with the Ku Klux Klan and everything else. Jones said there would be concentration camps and the government would do to us what Hitler did to the Jews. He made us truly believe that there would be a dictatorship and that fascism would take over," she recalled with a shudder.

Lena Pietila, who worked with Turner, Cobb, and the Millses at the Human Freedom deprogramming center, said that Jones would order his security cadre to carry out break-ins and so-called black bag jobs in order to support his claim to psychic powers. "They had people breaking into houses and reading their private records and personal documents and finding out all about them," said Pietila. "When they came into the Temple, the information was used as part of the 'revelations.'"

Exhaustion was yet another device in Jones's arsenal of behavioral controls. It was a fatigue caused not only by lack of sleep but by lack of food as well.

"The schools called up and asked why the kids were falling asleep in class and told us the kids were sick and needed to be eating meat," said Cobb. "The kids were falling asleep because they were being awakened at 5 A.M. every day and those who would not wake up were beaten until they did.

"In addition to this, you became your environment. We had five meetings a week for eight years, saying the same things over and over again. After all that, hey, you'd welcome death!"

7.

"A knife at the throat."

The night on the floor at the Weekend Discotheque passed without incident. I woke about 8 A.M., dirty and uncomfortable. We expected the Jonestown truck to pick us up early, but it didn't show up until about 10. We again loaded up and set out. Enroute, Ron Javers of the *Chronicle,* told me that something important had happened before we left Jonestown the previous night. He wouldn't tell me what it was because, whatever it was, Don Harris of NBC didn't want it to get out to the Concerned Relatives in our group. Javers assured me that I would find out in good time and I did: both Harris and Congressman Ryan had been given notes Friday night in the commune by people who wanted out.

The road was as muddy and rough as the day before. We got stuck and almost turned over halfway to Jonestown. But we got through and were met at Jonestown by Mark Lane, Charles Garry, and some of the young Temple people. Marceline Jones was there, telling us they had prepared a breakfast for us of pancakes and coffee. That raised my spirits

65

briefly. But Don Harris and the other newsmen vetoed breakfast. They said we didn't have time to eat.

We went to the pavilion, which would be packed with corpses within a few hours, and spent 15 minutes drinking coffee. Congressman Leo Ryan was there, continuing his interviews with followers of Jones. Jones, himself, was nowhere in sight. We were told he was sick and we might not see him that day. Don Harris vehemently protested and demanded of Lane that Jones appear for a filmed interview.

We started our daylight tour of Jonestown. We were assured by Lane and Temple leaders that we would be able to go anywhere in the settlement but that Marceline Jones wanted to first show us some of the model buildings.

She led us from the pavilion to a day care nursery for infants and young children. It was her special project. She was a registered nurse and had once been an inspector of day care facilities for the State of California. The Jonestown nursery was impressive. The large wooden building was spotless and contained an incubator, a respirator, a bright playroom, a nurse's office, cribs, and other modern equipment.

Our next stop was a classroom building for children with learning disabilities. The special education teacher there explained that she was able to give individual attention to each child unlike schools she had taught in in California.

Again, I was impressed.

Now the tour started to fall apart. Each newsman had his own idea of what he wanted to see next. All of us were getting a little restless about Marceline's guided tour. I decided to go off on my own to look for places where people actually lived. I suspected that the nursery and the classroom building were showplaces that didn't give a real pictures of the everyday life of people in the commune.

I had noticed three large wooden structures near the special education building that looked like residential dormitories. They had signs: Mary McLeod Bethune Terrace, Harriet Tubman Place, Jane Pittman Gardens. I headed for Jane Pittman Gardens. The shutters on all three buildings were closed tight. That caught my attention. As I got closer to Pittman Gardens, I could hear muffled coughs from inside. I knocked on the back door and no one answered. I tried to pull back a shutter for a look inside, but someone inside was holding on to it. I knocked again and then decided to go to the front entrance. I knocked on that door, but again no one answered. A young woman walking by came over and asked what I was doing. I told her I was curious about the dormitory and would like to see the inside. She said people might be resting but that she would find out. She told me to wait on the front porch while she went to the back. That seemed curious.

It was no surprise to me when she came back and said the people inside didn't want visitors. I smiled and she suggested that I go back to the main pavilion. She said she was sure I understood and I didn't answer. What I was thinking was that I had probably stumbled onto a warehouse for people the commune wanted kept out of sight, maybe people who had been tortured, beaten, or otherwise abused, as the Concerned Relatives had claimed.

I returned to the pavilion and told the other reporters there that we had to go back to Jane Pittman Gardens to find out what was going on there. Sarah Tropp, my friend of the night before, suddenly became very angry and said I had no right to invade the privacy of people in Jonestown. I told her that we had been assured we could see anything we wanted to see in the settlement and that I couldn't understand why a building was locked up and shuttered at noon on a Saturday.

Mike Prokes, a former television reporter with a CBS outlet in California, had joined the Temple several years before. He got into the conversation and agreed to go back and see if whoever was at Jane Pittman Gardens would let us inspect the building. All the newsmen, including the NBC crew, came along with Prokes. He identified himself, knocked on the door, and it was opened by a frail black woman who looked to be at least 70. He asked her if she wanted a television crew to come marching through the building. She said no, and closed the door.

Prokes said this proved that the people inside wanted no visitors. I said, "Bullshit." Then I told Prokes that he had framed the question to the old woman in a way calculated to get a negative answer, and that it was one thing to bring a television crew into a dormitory with lights and cameras, and another to let me go inside for a quiet talk. While we argued, Mark Lane and Charles Garry showed up, saying we could go in the building immediately.

No one had asked the people inside, but we entered anyway. The big room was filled with at least 100 bunk beds in long rows, with two or three feet between each bunk. Every bunk was occupied with an elderly woman, most of them black. The room was clean. The women seemed to have been well enough cared for and had been resting. I was told later that we had not been admitted originally because of the Temple's embarrassment at the overcrowding in the dormitory. I told Lane I understood the concern and could also understand the overcrowding.

We returned to the pavilion where Richard Tropp, the high school headmaster, was waiting. I asked him if he would take time to talk for a while. He agreed. What I wanted from Tropp was a profile of his own life so I could explain what had brought people like him to Guyana from the United States.

He told me he was 36 years old, had been born in Brooklyn, and had grown up on Long Island, where he had been president of his Temple youth group.

He had a B.A. from the University of Rochester and an M.A. in literature from the University of California at Berkeley. He had taught English at Fisk University, a black school in Nashville, Tennessee, and at Santa Rosa Junior College in California. He joined the Peoples Temple in 1970 while he was living in Redwood Valley, California. "I found out about this strange church that had white people and black people in it, with a swimming pool," he said. He said he had met Jones when he was working as a census taker. What struck him was that Jones had a son of his own and had adopted seven children, including a Korean and a black: "Good God, I thought, what is this?"

Tropp told me he became more and more involved with the Peoples Temple and that he and his wife had founded one of the Temple's first communes in Ukiah in 1973. Two years later, they moved to San Francisco when Jones decided he wanted to be closer to the blacks in the ghettoes there.

"Jones has always wanted to build a multi-racial, peaceful, egalitarian society," Tropp said. "Here we have the opportunity to create human institutions from cradle to grave, literally."

"Social change is really our focus. We don't see that religion and politics are separate. We feel that a lot of the opposition to us has been whipped up by conservative elements."

I asked him why Jones felt it necessary to leave the United States in June, 1977, just because of a critical article in *New West* magazine. Tropp denied that the article had caused Jones to go to Guyana. He said Jones had been planning the move to Jonestown "for a long time." It was Charles Garry, Tropp said, who advised Jones not to return to the States until various law suits were settled.

Why had Tropp come to Guyana without his wife? "Because," Tropp said, "I wanted to build, to validate this alternative. I feel a fulfillment for myself." He said he planned to stay at Jonestown indefinitely. I asked if he missed the U.S. His reply: "I've never been terribly fond of the United States since I was about 16 years old." He told me he had been involved in the civil rights and anti-Vietnam war movements, had become a dedicated Socialist, and saw the Peoples Temple as a living and working experiment in how society should work: "I think it's a tragedy we couldn't do it in the United States."

I asked him why he thought the Peoples Temple was under attack in the United States. Because, he said, "we believe there is some group, some force that is working to disrupt and agitate" against the Peoples Temple, which he described as a progressive Socialist institution. "We are not prepared to say who is doing it."

While talking to Tropp, I saw that Don Harris had started an interview with Jones. I decided to get in on it.

Harris had just asked him about the automatic weapon we had been told about by the Guyanese policeman the night before. Jones went into a rage: "A bold-faced lie," he declared. "It seems we're defeated by lies."

Harris then asked him about the beatings of Temple members we had been told about. "The beatings are not here," Jones said. "Yes, some people were spanked. I'm not going to deny it. But the mother demands it."

Then the question of John-John Stoen came up again. "I am John Stoen's father," Jones said. "Grace Stoen never showed any interest in him until all this came out in the press. . . . That (fathering John-John) is not one of the proudest things I've done."

He denied he had ever threatened anyone wanting to leave Jonestown, but "this is not a good time for black people in America."

He launched into a denunciation of the conspiracy to destroy him and his movement. "I wish somebody had shot me dead," he declared. "Now we've substituted the media smear for assassination."

Suddenly, the word came to us that several families had decided to leave with Ryan. People were gathering. Tension, for the first time, was so apparent that it could be felt.

Circumstances were pressing in. Facts were beginning to overcome Jones's denials as fast as he made them. Don Harris was throwing questions at him, hard questions that events were making even harder to answer.

"The more that leave, the less responsibility we have," Jones was saying, after denying that anyone wanted to leave the idyllic life Jonestown offered. "Who in the hell wants people?"

Harris returned to the question of guns at Jonestown. "This is rubbish. I'm defeated," Jones said, clearly near the breaking point. "I might as well die. The guns have never been used to intimidate people. Everyone is free to come and go. The only thing I feel is that everytime they go they lie. What I thought was keeping them here was the fear of the ghetto, alienation, the fear of industrialized society. I must have failed somehow. I want to hug them before they leave."

More people wanted to go. "I will let them. But they will try to destroy us. They'll try. They always lie when they leave," Jones said.

People were crying. Families were divided, with some members wanting to go and others not—or fearing they couldn't.

Patricia Parks, a settlement member, was resisting. She didn't want to go with her husband and her children. But she was finally persuaded to leave with them. She would be dead at the airstrip within a couple of hours.

Al Simons packed up his three kids and told Congressman Ryan that he was ready to leave.

Some of Jones's loyal followers moved in at this

point and started urging us to head down to the dump truck for the trip back to Port Kaituma. There was no violence or shoving, but the atmosphere was filled with tension.

I remember shaking hands with Marceline Jones and thanking her for the hospitality she had shown. I kissed Sarah Tropp good-bye and said I hoped we might one day meet again. As I started down the path leading from the pavilion to the truck, a woman appeared crying and screaming, "No, no, no!" It was Al Simons's wife.

John Jones, the adopted black son of Jim Jones, whispered to her: "Don't worry, we're going to take care of everything." He was in his early 20s and his remark seemed ominous.

Dick Dwyer, the man from the Embassy, Jackie Speier, Congressman Ryan, and Mark Lane realized that Al Simons's decision to leave was creating a custody problem. Ryan, Dwyer, and Lane went back to the pavilion with the Simons family to try to work it out. Jackie Speier and the rest of us got into the dump truck. It was about 2:45 P.M.

Within five minutes, we noticed a commotion in the pavilion. Don Harris, Tim Reiterman, Ron Javers, and I jumped off the truck and ran to investigate. We were stopped by Johnny Jones and other guards. They told us to stay where we were. Harris was allowed to proceed to the pavilion as our representative. He came back quickly to tell us that someone had tried to stab Congressman Ryan with a knife. Ryan soon appeared, walking with Dwyer toward the truck. Ryan's shirt and trousers were badly stained with blood, but he was unhurt.

He later told us that while talking to the Simons family and to Jones, a man came up behind him and put a knife to his throat. Ryan said he fell backward and Mark Lane grabbed the arm of the assailant, who was described as a powerful 35-year-old white man. As the man was disarmed, he was cut with his own knife and spurted blood on Ryan's clothes.

Lane and others persuaded Ryan to leave Jonestown after this incident, although he wanted to stay on and help resolve the Simonses dispute. Lane and Garry said they would stay behind to represent Mrs. Simon and the Temple in the custody fight and that Dwyer from the Embassy would remain to represent Al Simons.

As the dump truck started to pull out for the trip back to the airstrip, a short, slight blond-haired man jumped aboard with a small canvas bag in his hand. His name was Larry Layton.

The other defectors on the truck were frightened when Layton showed up. They said they couldn't believe he was a genuine defector. They said he would cause trouble.

I talked briefly with Layton on the ride back. He told me he was leaving because he thought Jim Jones had gone insane. He said he didn't want to say much more because he was very nervous.

The truth was that he had come to kill us.

I was about to learn things about the Peoples Temple I had never imagined. I was still unconvinced that it was the concentration camp its critics described, despite the defectors, despite the attempted stabbing of Ryan, and despite Jones strange behavior. But I wasn't sure.

8.

JONESTOWN:
"A feeling of freedom"

The pamphlet is full of smiling faces, of young and old, of black and white, of healthy looking tots napping on clean mattresses. On the cover is a young black boy smiling impishly, a monkey clinging to his tee shirt. The slick tract was titled "...a feeling of freedom" and it was Reverend Jim Jones's answer to his detractors about conditions in the Guyana jungle colony of Jonestown—his agrarian utopia.

Now that we know how it all ended at Jonestown, the public relations prose in the pamphlet resounds with a sense of ghoulish *double entendre.*

"Jonestown grows dearer to me each day. There is so much beauty, so much joy in the faces of our children and seniors," says Mary Lou Clancey as she peers out of the pages, smiling in a print summer dress.

"It's so peaceful and quiet here. At nighttime a person will feel comfortable knowing that they don't have to worry about being murdered or robbed in their sleep,— Scott Thomas."

"...Man, the Fillmore has seen the last of me!" bubbles ghetto youth Charles Wesley as he smiles into the camera.

Most poignant of all was the printed tribute of

paramedic trainee Marvin Sellers. "I'm going to school
and I actually like it. My teachers are Sharon Swaney
(R.N., P.M.P.), Joyce Parks (R.N., F.N.P.)...and Dr.
Schacht (M.D.).

It was Dr. Lawrence Schacht who reportedly mixed
the poisonous punch with which hundreds of members of
the Peoples Temple followed the Reverend Jim Jones to
oblivion in Guyana on November 18.

*"Impressive work,—Officer in charge of Guyana,
Jamaica, Trinidad, and Tobago, U. S. State Department."*

*"Peace and love in action—Minister of Foreign
Affairs, Guyana."*

In May, 1978 Kathy Hunter, a 58-year-old freelance
writer from Ukiah, the first California site of the Peoples
Temple, went to Guyana to interview Reverend Jones, to
visit the widely-touted agrarian community he founded,
and to find out the truth about conflicting claims.

She met three aides of Jones in Georgetown on May
17. "At first, everything was lovey-dovey, but when I told
them I wanted an interview with Reverend Jim Jones alone
and in person, the chill set in," she recounted. "Then I said
I wanted to talk to each of the relatives alone and
outside—where we couldn't be overheard."

The conversation became heated. One of the Jones
aides finally hissed: "Newspaper and television reporters
are bad."

Strangely, Mrs. Hunter found her visa reduced by the
Guyana government from 11 days to one. She was told to
leave on the next outgoing plane. The government of
Guyana provided her with an armed guard when she
voiced suspicions that Temple members might be waiting
to kill her on her way to the airport.

Mrs. Hunter returned to Ukiah where her husband,
George, was executive editor of the *Ukiah Daily Journal*
and an account of her ordeal was published. It was not
long before what was described as the "campaign" began.
Two men broke into the family home one Sunday
afternoon, according to the Hunters, grabbed the writer,
and forced part of a bottle of whiskey down her throat.
She was briefly hospitalized.

Her brother Michael, a Legal Service Foundation legal assistant in Ukiah, found a note in his car formed by letters cut out of the newspapers. "Hey, white trash . . . we know where you live! We're watching you all the time, we know where you work, we know your home number, we know your trashy life, honkey . . . you drives your dead mama's car . . . keep your ass clean and your mouth clammed (sic) up . . ." the note said.

Kathy Hunter felt she knew from where the harrassment was coming. But she could find no proof.

Nonetheless, the Peoples Temple issued a press release on June 12, 1978, charging: "Kathy Hunter misrepresented herself to gain entry into the country . . . She refused every invitation to visit the Jonestown project once she was in the country . . . Moreover, it is hardly likely that Mrs. Hunter came to Guyana as an independent, freelance journalist travelling on her own, as the media has portrayed." Temple officials charged that Mrs. Hunter and "even more segments of the media are involved with . . . [a] monstrous conspiracy" against the Temple.

Of still more damaging impact was the affidavit of Deborah Blakey which described not only the deterioration of Jones and the Temple, as was previously mentioned, but made an unsparingly specific critique of the Jonestown mission. Blakey's account received heavy coverage in the San Francisco press, following as it did the opening salvo in *New West* and the ensuing stories in the city papers.

She had been sent to Guyana, a trusted member of the congregation, and, after a week in Georgetown, went to the Jonestown mission.

"Conditions at Jonestown were even worse than I had feared they would be," she later wrote. "The settlement was swarming with armed guards. No one was permitted to leave unless on a special assignment and those assignments were given only to the most trusted. We were allowed to associate with Guyanese people only while on a "mission."

The panorama opened up before Deborah Blakey in chilling detail. She watched the Temple members labor in the fields 11 hours a day, six days a week, and also on Sunday from 7 A.M. to 2 P.M. Breaks, other than lunch, were frowned upon. There would be rice for breakfast, she related, and rice water soup for lunch and rice with beans for dinner. On Sundays, each member received an egg and a cookie. Twice or three times a week, there were vegetables.

By February of 1978, Deborah, along with half of the colony, had sever diarrhea and high fever. "Like most of the other sick people, I was not given any nourishing foods to help recover. I was given water and a tea drink until I was well enough to return to the basic rice and beans diet."

Jones, on the other hand, dined out of his own refrigerator. He ate meat regularly from his well-stocked larder. He claimed to be having problems with his blood sugar. The two women with whom he lived and the two boys, including young John Stoen, dined with the membership, but, as Deborah reported, "were in much better physical shape than everyone else, since they were also allowed to eat the food in Reverend Jones's refrigerator.

As for outside visitors, Blakey said, their presence—which was permitted rarely—became the occasions for remarkable communal performances, as in the case of the Ryan mission. "Before the visitor arrived, Reverend Jones would instruct us on the image we were to project. The workday would be shortened. The food would be better. Sometimes there would be music and dancing. Aside from these performances, there was little joy or hope in any of our lives. An air of despondency prevailed."

Talk of death was constant. On this point, the Blakey affidavit became prophetic.

"In Jonestown, the concept of mass suicide for socialism arose. Because our lives were so wretched anyway, and because we were so afraid to contradict Reverend Jones, the concept was not challenged."

Then came an episode that Blakey said "convinced me that Reverend Jones had sufficient control over the minds of the residents that it would be possible for him to effect a mass suicide." These words were written five months before Jones actually did order that unimaginable event, one which stunned the credulity of everyone in the world with access to radio, television, newspapers, or whatever other means exists for conveying news.

What Jones did was reenact the ritual suicide. He declared a "white night"—a state of emergency. Sirens blared as the population of Jonestown rushed to assembly. As was customary on such alerts, the security force armed themselves with rifles, moving through the community to make sure everyone was responding.

On this occasion, Jones informed the community that "our situation had become hopeless and that the only course of action open to us was a mass suicide for the glory of socialism.

"We were told that we would be tortured by mercenaries if we were taken alive. Everyone, including the children, was told to line up. As we passed through the line, we were given a small glass of red liquid to drink. We were told that the liquid contained poison and that we would die within 45 minutes. We all did as we were told."

As in earlier suicide drills in San Francisco, the episode was, in that case, just a ruse. It had been intended, Jones said, as a loyalty test. But then Jones issued his awesome sentence. "He warned us that the time was not far off when it would become necessary for us to die by our own hands," Blakey said.

So wretched had life become for the young woman and so great the sheer pain of physical exhaustion that, in her own words, "This event was not traumatic for me. I had become indifferent as to whether I lived or died."

Nonetheless, in April she was reassigned to Georgetown and began to plan her escape.

Surreptitiously, Deborah contacted her sister who wired her a ticket. She then sought the help of the U. S. Embassy to arrange her departure from Guyana. This was a stage of her escape that she found terrifying. Jones had boasted that he had a spy in the U.S. Embassy who would immediately let him know if anyone came there to seek help. She expressed public gratitude to two members of the American mission, Richard McCoy and Daniel Weber, for their help.

Nonetheless, Jones was at this time using the official reports of the U.S. Embassy in Guyana to refute charges by the Concerned Relatives of brutal work and living conditions in the colony.

In a press release containing the verse of Matthew on its letterhead: ("For I was an hungered and ye gave me meat; I was thirsty and ye gave me drink . . .") the Temple quoted from the State Department report.

"As part of the traditional and internationally-sanctioned protection services, officers of the American Embassy in Georgetown, Guyana, periodically visit the People's Agricultural Temple located at Jonestown, Guyana. These officers have been free to move about the grounds and speak privately to any individuals, including persons who were believed by their family and friends to be held against their will."

Tiny and perhaps unimportant as Guyana was, the State Department reporting from Georgetown might have qualified as one of the most egregious intelligence snafus of the year. A far cry from the Cold War days in 1964 when the American CIA and British Intelligence deftly colluded to support the victory of Prime Minister Forbes Burnham over the impetuous leftist Cheddi Jagan. But, then again, was it the role of the U.S. Government in the post-Nixon years to monitor the activities of American citizens conducting themselves in what seemed to be a peaceable manner?

9.

*"In the jungle, a press card is just
another piece of paper."*

We reached the Port Kaituma airstrip at 4:15 P.M. In
a few minutes, it would run with blood.

The trip back in the dump truck had been more
uncomfortable this last time. We had 16 extra people
aboard—the Parks and Boggs families, Vernon
Gosney, Monica Bagby, and Larry Layton. Layton
turned out to be our enemy within. But the rest were
all genuine Jonestown defectors who had chosen to
leave with Congressman Leo J. Ryan. Jones had
given them their passports and 5,000 Guyanese
dollars to buy passage home.

Anthony Katsaris, tall, good-looking and quiet,
was tearful as we made our way toward the airstrip.
He had failed to persuade his sister, Maria, to return
to California with him. I wanted to comfort him, but
there was nothing to say.

In my mind, Anthony was not one of the crazies
among the Concerned Relatives. He and his father,
who was with the group back at the Pegasus Hotel,
had not dwelled on tales of abuse and terror at
Jonestown. They simply wanted Maria to come

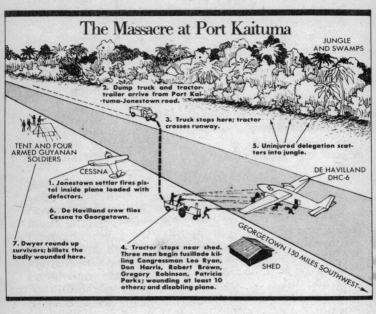

The Massacre at Port Kaituma

JUNGLE AND SWAMPS

2. Dump truck and tractor-trailer arrive from Port Kaituma-Jonestown road.

3. Truck stops here; tractor crosses runway.

5. Uninjured delegation scatters into jungle.

TENT AND FOUR ARMED GUYANAN SOLDIERS

CESSNA

DE HAVILLAND DHC-6

1. Jonestown settler fires pistol inside plane loaded with defectors.

6. De Havilland crew flies Cessna to Georgetown.

7. Dwyer rounds up survivors; billets the badly wounded here.

4. Tractor stops near shed. Three men begin fusillade killing Congressman Leo Ryan, Don Harris, Robert Brown, Gregory Robinson, Patricia Parks; wounding at least 10 others; and disabling plane.

GEORGETOWN 150 MILES SOUTHWEST

SHED

home. I thought Maria, at 25, was old enough to make her own decisions. If she wanted to stay at the Temple and share a bed with Jim Jones, that was her business. The people at the Temple had let Anthony try to talk her out of it. It wasn't Jim Jones's fault or Anthony's that she chose to stay.

Yet I liked Anthony and was sad for him. He obviously loved his sister and desperately wanted her back in Northern California where their mother lived with their father, a principal of a school for emotionally disturbed children. He had once been a Greek Orthodox priest.

All in all, however, the trip back to the airstrip was relaxed in spite of everything, including the attempt on Ryan's life at Jonestown and the apparent paranoia of the defecting families who kept telling us that Layton was up to no good.

I remember putting my arm around Jackie Speier and telling her we ought to have a reunion someday back in Washington and invite the other newsmen on this trip. I had come to like them, despite initial feelings that they were treating me as an outsider. I had also come to like Ryan, despite my general skepticism about politicians. He had won my respect on this trip as a decent, caring man. I was convinced he had gone to Jonestown, at some personal risk, because of his concern for the people there, not as a publicity stunt.

So things seemed well with the world, although I still thought this adventure into the wilds of Guyana was the craziest story I had ever covered during my six years as a reporter at *The Washington Post*. The first two days at Georgetown had been an amusing and bizarre circus, with Ryan in the center ring. But the two days at Jonestown put it in a different light. It was coming out as a human and humane quest for whatever the truth might be about this strange flock of Californians transplanted in the wilderness.

I had decided to write a long and thoughtful piece about Ryan and Jonestown, trying to explain the

complicated motivations and convictions of everyone involved—Ryan, the defectors, the Tropps, the
Peoples Temple movement, and the ideals and
reality of Jonestown as I then perceived it. I
anticipated trouble convincing my editors that the
big story was not the knife assault on Ryan. That
seemed to me to have been an aberration, the work
of one unstable individual. It was not all that
surprising, either, in a community that was in part a
salvage operation for drug addicts, prostitutes, the
sick, and the disturbed flotsam from the underclass
of American society. I was determined to resist any
scoop mentality in Washington that would force me
to begin and end my story with the attempt on Ryan's
life. Maybe I could do a piece on that incident and
follow up with a big analysis of Jonestown itself.

The truth was that I rather admired Jim Jones's
goals. I was convinced that Jones was very sick,
both physically and mentally. But the Peoples
Temple hadn't struck me as a crazy fringe cult, like
the Moonies or whoever they are who try to stick
flowers in your lapel at every airport in America.

It seemed to me that the Peoples Temple had a
legitimate purpose, a noble purpose, and was more
or less succeeding. The fact that 16 people, most of
them members of two families, were homesick and
leaving with Ryan didn't change that view.

I suspected that the big story for the San
Francisco papers would be a sensational account of
Ryan's brush with death in Jonestown. But to me,
the experience we had been through was more
profound and complicated than that. No one, not
even the defectors on our truck, had offered any
proof that the 900 or so people at Jonestown were
being starved, mistreated, or held against their will.
Jones and his followers had certainly put the best
light on things and had exaggerated some of their
triumphs. I didn't believe, for example, that there
were 1,200 people at Jonestown despite Jones's
claim. Nor did I believe that enough land was being

GUYANA
MASSACRE

PHOTOGRAPHS AND COMMENTARY
BY
FRANK JOHNSTON

Congressman Leo J. Ryan
James K. W. Atherton
© 1976, *THE WASHINGTON POST*

Reverend Jim Jones
© 1977, *ASSOCIATED PRESS*

After the ambush, Chuck Krause returned to Georgetown to file his exclusive account of the massacre at Port Kaituma.

Forty-eight hours after the shooting, a hat, a box of matches, blood stains, and a plane with a flat tire and a few bullet holes were the only evidence of the incident.

Flying into Jonestown, it looked like a county fair. Then we realized that all those people weren't moving. It was as if time had stopped.

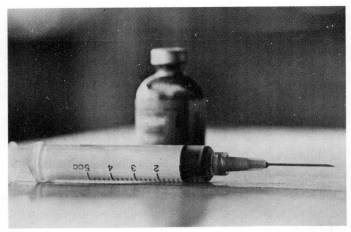

Liquid Valium and cyanide were strewn all over the table in the medical tent. On a counter a hypodermic needle was left. The evidence at the scene gave no immediate reason for the use of hypodermics.

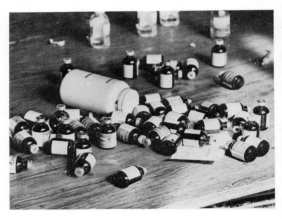

I walked down the path to a vat filled with a vile-looking
reddish-purple liquid. I was told that the people had been
poisoned.

Most of the bodies were lying face down. This was when I realized that children were among the dead.

Nothing escaped.

Everywhere I turned, I saw bodies. I was overwhelmed by the scope of the carnage. Somehow, nametags were tied to the wrist or ankle of many of the victims.

Ironically, a clock stopped around the time the suicides occurred. Letters and children's drawings were other mute witnesses.

A cache of firearms and a trunk full of American passports
were recovered by the Guyanese police.

Guyanese Army soldiers shared my revulsion at the stench of death.

The Reverend Jones's throne stood empty, surrounded by the bodies of his followers. Above it, the inscription struck me as the final irony.

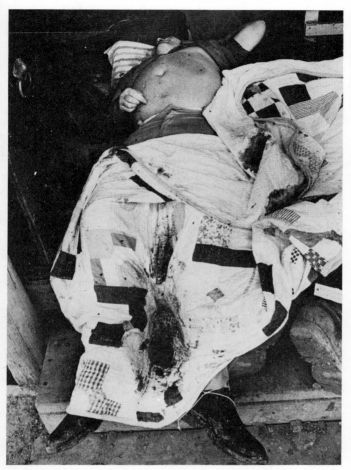

On the steps of his throne room, the leader lay dead.

cultivated to provide his followers regularly with the kind of food we had been served. But those things seemed relatively minor in the context of the far more serious allegations against the Temple that we had been unable to verify.

Edith Parks, one of the defectors on the truck, even told me she would probably return to Jonestown after seeing her family in California. The hundreds of people still at Jonestown, who had chosen not to defect, seemed ample proof that they were relatively content.

Ryan had given them every chance to leave with him. Representatives of the U.S. Embassy and the Guyanese government had been there to offer further assurances that they had a way out. Any attempt to prevent people from leaving would have been reported in the national and world press, spread all over television and denounced by Ryan himself. We were a long way from civilization. But in my naive view at that moment, it seemed that the communications systems and jet aircraft we were accustomed to provided the shield from harm those people needed. I was also convinced, naively, that there was nothing Jim Jones or his followers, Larry Layton included, could do to us. After all, we represented insitutions of great "power"—the press, the U.S. Congress, the State Department, the government of Guyana.

It didn't occur to me until later that "power" in this context is a myth. We had no arsenal of guns. Georgetown, with its telex machines and telephones and troops, was far away. We were in the jungle where a press card was just another piece of paper. Jim Jones had the power here. He could stop us simply by having us killed. The thought that he might try never crossed my mind.

I assumed that his response to our visit, if any, would be a campaign by the Peoples Temple in Guyana and San Francisco to discredit Ryan and the defectors who had left with us.

Jones had already set the stage for that, saying that all those who deserted him were liars. He would accuse them of stealing money or would produce documents in which they had admitted criminal acts or abberational behavior. The defectors never said that such documents were forged but that they had been signed as a test of loyalty to the Temple. Most of the documents I was aware of had been signed while the Temple members were in the United States. I found it difficult to accept the idea that grown people, many of them well-educated, would sign false documents.

During the 80-minute ride from Jonestown to the airstrip, Larry Layton told me in a brief conversation that he had decided to leave with us because terrible things were happening at the Temple. But none of the other defectors on the truck and none of the people at the commune had confirmed any of the horror stories we had gotten from the Concerned Relatives back at Georgetown.

As I got off the dump truck for the last time, I was wondering how I could explain all this in a newspaper story. My mind was also on the trip back to the hotel where I would get a good meal and my first shower and shave in more than 24 hours. I thought maybe I could leave the next day for Trinidad, check into a good hotel with a beach, write my Peoples Temple saga, and try to leave for the States on Wednesday, November 11. That would get me home for Thanksgiving.

We jumped off the truck and unloaded all the gear—television equipment and the trunks and suitcases brought along by the defectors. Ryan agreed to tell us about the incident with the knife back at Jonestown. He had made the return trip in the cab of the truck, so we didn't have the details of the incident.

Ryan sat down in a shed at the side of the airstrip and waited until the NBC television crew could set up. The crew included cameramen Bob Brown and

Steve Sung, correspondent Don Harris, and producer Bob Flick. Ron Javers, Tim Reiterman, and I were the "print" journalists. Greg Robinson, a *San Francisco Examiner* photographer, snapped pictures of the Congressman, sitting there in his bloodstained shirt and trousers.

He told us that the night before he and Don Harris had been given notes indicating that some of the Jonestown people wanted to leave. "All of a sudden," he said, "there were whole families that wanted out. We made some arrangements to do it."

The logistics were difficult because charter planes were scarce in Guyana. He had arranged through the Embassy in Georgetown to get two aircraft to Port Kaituma. They had a total of 24 seats. That meant four or five of us would have to spend another night in Port Kaituma because Ryan had promised the defectors they would be on the first flights out.

Ryan then reviewed the scene we had witnessed from a distance that afternoon when Al Simon wanted to leave Jonestown with his three children and his father against the wishes of his wife. Ryan, Richard Dwyer of the Embassy, and the Temple lawyers, Mark Lane and Charles Garry, tried to work out some arrangement over the custody of the three Simon children. "Everything was going fine," Ryan was telling us, when "the whole atmosphere became distinctly hostile and tense in a quiet sort of way ... All of a sudden a very strong man had his arm around my neck and a very sharp knife at my throat."

Ryan said he leaned away from the knife blade and fell backward on top of his assailant, whom he described as a powerfully-built white man, about six feet tall, between 35 and 40 years old. His attacker never got a firm grip on him, Ryan said, People then intervened, including Mark Lane, "who probably did more to save my life any anyone else." During the struggle, Ryan's assailant was cut with the knife and his blood spurted onto Ryan's clothing.

Charles Garry, the Temple's other lawyer, was "terribly apologetic" about the incident, Ryan said.

The Congressman was "shaken up pretty badly" by the incident, but said he had been willing to stay at Jonestown to resolve the custody dispute in the Simons family. But it was decided that Dwyer, representing the Embassy, would see us off at the airport and then return to Jonestown to settle the matter with Lane and Garry. The two lawyers had promised Ryan that nothing would happen to the Simons family while Dwyer was gone.

Ryan also told us as we sat in the shed by the airstrip that in addition to the 16 Jonestown defectors who were going back with us, three other communards had escaped that morning and apparently were making their way through the jungle to Port Kaituma.

We finished our conversation with Ryan and he went out with Jackie Speier to figure out who was going back on the two airplanes that just landed. One of the planes was a 19 passenger twin Otter, the other was a small, single engine craft that could carry five passengers. The Otter was the same plane that had brought us down the day before and had the same pilot, Guy Spence. He parked the aircraft by the shed, halfway down the runway. The smaller plane was parked about 30 feet away. At the far end of the runway was a third plane, a Guyanese military aircraft that had broken a wheel and was being repaired. It was guarded by four Guyanese soldiers. A crowd of townspeople was also on hand for the rare experience of watching a takeoff at the remote airstrip.

The time was now 4:25 P.M.

Jackie Speier was standing between the two planes with the Jonestown defectors. She was trying to sort out which of them would go on which plane. She didn't want to split families. For the first flight out she picked five for the small plane, not including Larry Layton. He became angry and argued that

Ryan had promised him he would be on the first
flight. Jackie told him the second flight would leave
in a few minutes with him aboard. But Layton
insisted on appealing to Ryan for a place on the
small plane. Ryan told Jackie to put Layton on the
first flight.

The small plane was loaded, Layton aboard.
Jackie, Tim Reiterman, and I gathered with some
others at the door of the larger plane. Ryan wanted
all of the Peoples Temple defectors to be frisked for
weapons, a precaution that seemed unecessary to
me. But I helped with that chore. We found no guns.

Jackie meanwhile had the job of deciding who
was going to stay behind. The plane wouldn't hold
all of us. The defectors had first priority, so either
some newsmen or some of the Concerned Relatives
were going to miss the flight.

Reiterman and I started lobbying with Jackie. We
told her we had to get back to file our stories that
night about the attempted assault on Ryan. In my
case, that wasn't entirely true, although I did want to
get in touch with my paper in Washington to explain
how I thought the story should be handled—without
sensationalism.

Jackie never had time to make that decision.
Someone was shouting, "Hey, look over there."
Across the runway, about 300 yards away, the
Jonestown dump truck and the tractor, pulling a flat
bed trailer, had driven up. People were getting off
the vehicles. Our defectors were frightened and a
sense of urgency developed immediately about
getting them aboard the Otter. Their first reaction
was that the arrivals from the Temple had come to
keep them from leaving.

Just then Dwyer, who had gone into Port Kaituma
a few minutes before, drove up in another truck,
accompanied by a local policeman carrying a
shotgun.

From across the runway, three of the new
Jonestown arrivals—all men—came striding toward

us. I didn't see any weapons. I thought they might start a fistfight. But I wasn't overly concerned since the local police were there. I wanted to take in whatever might happen next. I figured the men would first approach Ryan and perhaps deliver some message from Jones protesting the departure of the defectors.

The three men walked up to our group. I got out of the way and moved back to the door of the plane with Jackie Speier. Bob Brown and Steve Sung trained the cameras on the three men as they pushed some of the Guyanese bystanders back toward the edge of the runway. They took the policeman's shotgun and he backed away.

The tractor, towing the trailer, had now moved up between our two planes. The smaller plane started to taxi down the runway in the direction of the parked dump truck.

The shooting started then. People were yelling. I dropped my notebook and ran around the tail of the plane, away from the noise. I passed the NBC crew who were filming as they edged back toward the tail. I dove behind a wheel to put the plane between me and the gunmen. Somebody else was already there. I still don't know who it was.

The shots were louder and closer now. Someone landed on top of me and rolled off. I could feel dirt spraying over me but there were no screams or moans. Just the pop-pop-pop of the bullets. The shots were coming from one side of me and from the rear and I knew I was on the wrong side of the plane. Suddenly, my left hip burned and I felt a tooth chip. I knew I had been hit.

I was thinking this is crazy. It couldn't be. It was going to die in the middle of the jungle, in Guyana, so far away from my family and friends. I thought about the coming Thanksgiving. I wasn't going to be there. I was going to be dead. It was all so unfair, so unjust, so ironic. I was here working. I had nothing to do with the Peoples Temple. I did not want to destroy it. I hadn't believed it was what its detractors said it was. How stupid, I was thinking. How Goddamn stupid I had been.

Another body flew on top of me and rolled off. I was helpless. I lay there behind the plane's wheel, which no longer offered protection. I lay still, hoping they would think I was dead. But I knew that blood wasn't pouring out of me. I tried not to breathe. I waited for a big bullet to come crashing into my back. I was waiting to die. I became resigned. O.K., I was ready. Let's just have it quick. Quick.

A few seconds passed. No shots. Then a volley of three more. Where were they? What was going on? I was afraid to look, to move, to think. Suddenly I was aware that the plane's engines were revving up.

I peeked under my arm down the runway. I could see the tractor parked there. Now was my chance. If this plane was going, I was going to be on it.

I ran around to the front of the plane to wave to the pilot. Then I dashed toward the door. It was closed, but the cargo hatch was open. Jackie Speier was there, hanging on. Anthony Katsaris was on the ground, bleeding badly. I told Jackie to get in. She told me she was hurt bad. I saw that her arm was nearly torn apart and was bleeding badly. I grabbed her and threw her on the plane. I tried to pick up Anthony, but I couldn't manage. I was sorry. But I jumped through the cargo door and pulled it shut.

Jackie was crumpled in the corner, gushing blood. She asked me if Leo Ryan was okay. I said I didn't know. She told me she thought she was going to die. I tore off my shirt and tried to make a bandage. I was holding onto the door, half afraid that I would be sucked out of the plane when it began its takeoff. I yelled for the co-pilot who was in the cabin.

But the plane couldn't move. One tire had been shot out. One engine had been damaged by the gunfire. The cabin with crowded with defectors, lying on the floor. They were uninjured.

The co-pilot told us to get out of the plane. We had

no idea if the Jonestown gunmen would return. The defectors, terror-stricken, ran toward the jungle along the airstrip once the door was opened.

I saw Richard Dwyer of the Embassy standing with Bob Flick near the shed. Dwyer's pants were bloody. He had been hit in the thigh but he seemed okay. I ran over to them, scared and confused, yelling, "Mr. Dwyer!"

He replied: "Why don't you just call me Dick?"

10.

"Let me make it through the night."

I stood there a moment with Dick Dwyer and Bob Flick, then turned and looked back toward the plane. I saw for the first time the dimensions of the slaughter, the enormity of the horror on this remote jungle airstrip.

Seven bodies lay under and around the big plane. They were covered with blood. Greg Robinson lay near the wheel with the blown out tire. He was face down, one leg drawn up under him, his camera still around his neck. Dead.

A woman lay on her back near the door. I learned later it was Patricia Parks, who had defected from Jonestown that day. Dead.

Anthony Katsaris lay where I had left him, near the cargo door and the body of Mrs. Parks. Badly wounded.

Behind the tail lay Bob Brown, the NBC cameraman who had joked and laughed his way through the trip. He had taken to calling me Ralph because of my Polo jeans with the name of designer Ralph Lauren on them. Dead. His brains were blown out and scattered beside his body on the runway. The blue NBC mini-camera was beside him, its rubber electrical cord leading to his film technician, Steve Sung. Sung writhed in pain. He was badly wounded.

Under the plane, near the wheel at which I had sought protection, was the long, lean body of Don Harris, the NBC correspondent who had fired questions at Jim Jones only hours before. He was on his back. Dead, only two feet from where I had been.

On the other side of the wheel, a foot-and-a-half from where I had played dead, was Congressman Leo Ryan. He was on his side, arms thrust out in front of him. Dead. His head was covered with blood.

The Jonestown gunmen had done their work well, calmly shooting the wounded after they had fallen. How I missed death, I'll never know.

I turned to Bob Flick, the kind and sensitive NBC producer. I felt like I was going to cry. But I noticed that he had tears in his eyes as he looked at his crew—two of them dead, the other badly wounded. I thought he was about to break down. But this was no time to feel sorry for myself. My hip was hurting from a grazing wound, but I knew I was lucky and all right.

I walked around for a bit to get hold of myself. There were things to be done. Jackie was in the plane, wounded and bleeding badly. Anthony was there, also wounded. Steve Sung looked like he might not live. Someone had to help Dwyer, who had taken command and was asking that we move the wounded into the nearby brush. He feared the gunmen would return to finish us off.

A crowd of Guyanese began to gather. We asked them for help. The local police arrived, explaining that they had been helpless after their only armed officer was disarmed by the Jonestown killers. They had obviously fled when the trouble started. Now they were offering to set up a roadblock and radio Georgetown for help. Their offer of assistance was small comfort.

We got Jackie, Steve, and Anthony into the brush.

Ron Javers and Tom Reiterman joined us. Javers had a bullet in his shoulder blade. Reiterman was bleeding from wounds in the arm. When the shooting had started, they ran around the plane as I had, and then raced across the runway into the brush. They had made crude tourniquets and bandages for themselves and were now ready to pitch in as best they could.

There was no panic among us, then or later. We feared, sensibly, that the Jonestown assassination squad would be back. Vehicles occasionally approached the runway, police cars, for example. Every time we heard a motor, we ran into the bush. We saw no sign of the promised police road block and, in any case, didn't trust the police. We didn't expect them to harm us. But we didn't expect them to protect us if the Jonestown squad reappeared. They had run away the first time.

We moved the wounded away from the plane, giving them water and rum as a painkiller. Dwyer was talking to the pilot, Guy Spence, who was unhurt. Spence said he was radioing Georgetown for help and later said he had gotten through, although I had my doubts. The police also promised us that they had notified Georgetown and that there would be a Guyanese military plane at the airstrip within an hour.

That seemed doubtful. It was now nearly 6 P.M. and it would be dark by the time a plane could arrive at the unlighted runway.

I suddenly became aware that the small plane was still sitting at the end of the runway. I asked Dwyer if any of those people had been shot. He said he didn't know and a few minutes later we walked toward it. Just then the plane started taxiing down the runway with its pilot, Tommy Fernandez, at the controls. Our own pilot, Guy Spence, was in the co-pilot's seat, waving us out of the way. We turned and ran, thinking Spence meant that another attack from Jonestown was about to begin. But they were deliberately leaving us to our fate, abandoning the seriously wounded.

"Those fuckers," I said to Dwyer. "They've left us here and didn't even take the wounded."

No one had spoken to the four Guyanese soldiers at the end of the runway. They sat by, not lifting a hand, while we were being shot. Flick told us that when the assault began he had run to the soldiers' tent and pleaded for help. They had refused, saying it was a fight between Americans. They wanted nothing to do with it. Flick demanded that they lend him a gun. They refused again and then stood by to let the Jonestown truck and tractor pass after the shooting was all over. So much for the Guyanese Army.

It was getting dark, but we still had some hope that a plane from Georgetown might be on its way. We tried to minister to the wounded. Several times, hearing engines, we faded into the bush. At one point, all the Guyanese bystanders started running away. It was a false alarm, but their panic infected some of our Jonestown defectors and Concerned Relatives. Six of them ran into the jungle and kept going—Jim Cobb, Tina Turner, Chris O'Neill, Tom Bogue, Brenda and Tracy Parks. They were not found for several days.

Steve Sung was getting delirious. We kept giving him rum and whiskey as a sedative but he was still crying with pain. Finally he fell asleep.

I started walking back to our disabled plane and ran into Dale Parks, one of the Jonestown defectors. He had been on the small plane when the shooting started. He told me excitedly that the short, slightly-built blonde man who was standing 20 feet away talking with two Guyanese policemen was the man who had tried to kill the passengers on the small plane. It was Larry Layton. There was something about Parks's urgency and fright that told me he was probably telling the truth.

I went to Dwyer and told him the story. He and I

walked over to Layton and told the policemen that we wanted him taken into custody. They seemed reluctant and Layton mumbled something about not doing anything wrong.

But Dwyer wouldn't let it drop. I am convinced now that his strength and bravery during the coming night of pain and terror saved us all. And now he was facing Layton and the policemen in an imperious manner. He pointed out coldly that he was the chief of mission of the U.S. Embassy in Georgetown and he demanded that Layton be arrested. The Guyanese were impressed. They took Larry Layton, under arrest, into Port Kaituma.

Layton would later be charged with five counts of murder and two counts of attempted murder. According to Dale Parks, he had opened fire with a revolver as the small plane was trying to take off at the start of the attack. He had shot Monica Bagby and Vernon Gosney before his gun jammed and Parks was able to wrestle it away from him. It's a mystery why Layton stayed behind with us rather than escaping with the other Jonestown gunmen. My only guess was that he was waiting for another chance to shoot some of us.

Dwyer got involved with another problem. At his request, the police had driven their Land Rover into Port Kaituma to bring back the local nurse. They returned, saying she refused to come to the airstrip. Dwyer told them to go back and get some pain pills from her. They refused unless one of us went into town with them. That was absolutely unacceptable to Dwyer for two reasons. First, we still thought the Jonestown gunmen were regrouping nearby. Second, we didn't know who was and who wasn't a policeman. In Port Kaituma, the police neither carry identification cards nor wear uniforms.

Dwyer again played commander-in-chief. Get some pills, he told the Guyanese in the firmest way. They left again. Before long, all the Guyanese were referring to Dwyer as "The Ambassador." The

Temple defectors called him "Deputy Ambassador."

At our first meeting at the embassy in George-town, Dwyer had greeted me with an unpleasant "Oh, I've heard about you." He was a big, heavy set man in his mid-50s. He was clearly not delighted with Ryan's visit or the problems created by the newsmen in the party.

But here at the airstrip, in our time of trouble, he came through as a rock of strength and sanity. I am not particularly jingoistic but damn it, I thought, if there ever was a time for an American diplomat to kick some ass and stop pretending the United States is a powerless little country sandwiched between Canada and Mexico, this was it. Dwyer was kicking ass. Beautifully.

It was almost 8 P.M. This awful, endless day had turned into a black and moonless night. The time had come to ask for help from the Guyanese soldiers at the end of the runway. We had badly wounded people on our hands. We couldn't leave them out in the bush all night for the ants to feed on. Jackie Speier, Steve Sung, Anthony Katsaris, and Vernon Gosney needed shelter and protection. The soldiers had guns and a tent.

Dwyer went down to talk to them. They agreed to let us use their cots as stretchers to bring the wounded to their tent, a distance of 400 to 500 yards. One of the townspeople helped bring the cots to us.

The journey to the army tent was painful for our wounded and difficult for us but we had no choice. We loaded them, trying to be gentle, and carried them to the end of the runway where the tent sat near the single road leading to Port Kaituma and Jonestown. If the Jonestown gunmen returned, they would have to wipe out the soldiers before proceeding down the runway. So it was more dangerous, in a sense, for the wounded to be in their tent. But the troops had automatic weapons and we hoped they would defend themselves and the wounded if an attack occurred.

The soldiers were jumpy and I was afraid they might shoot one of us in the dark. Dwyer shared that fear and arranged for us to use a code word we could shout from a distance when approaching the tent. The word was "Demerara," the name of one of Guyana's rivers. Bob Flick offered to supply the soldiers with strobe lights to illuminate the tent area. They declined. They didn't want a bright target for the Jonestown crowd.

Dwyer decided that the rest of us would be better off some place other than the airstrip. So we arranged to spend the night at a little bar called the Rum House, about 600 yards from the end of the runway.

The local police said they would guard the bar against an attack, which they and other townspeople, as well as our Jonestown defectors, expected. The rest of us were unsure. They could have finished all of us off that afternoon. But we were frightened and probably most of us were in shock. We had not eaten since being served cheese sandwiches at Jonestown at noon. Water was scarce and reserved mainly for the wounded. We were alone and cut off in one of the most remote parts of the world, surrounded—so we thought—by killer squads from the Jones's Temple who might at any minute return. We didn't know if any word of our troubles had reached Georgetown and the outside world. And, as the hours passed, it was increasingly unlikely that the promised Guyanese military plane would arrive. We had survived one nightmare and now, defenseless in the jungle, another was beginning.

Dwyer and some of the other survivors walked down to the Rum House to make the necessary arrangements and to ask the police to post their guards. I stayed with Ron Javers, the *San Francisco Chronicle* reporter, who was at the tent with a bullet in his shoulder. He and I did what we could for the more badly wounded, who were lying on the dirt floor. We gave them water, rum, and the pain pills we had finally obtained from the nurse in Port Kaituma. There was no food. There was little else we could do to make them comfortable.

For awhile, Javers and I sat outside the tent with the soldiers. Neville Annibourne, the Guyanese information officer who had been with us at Jonestown, was there, too. The soldiers had little to say. Annibourne was apologetic about everything and offered me some of the rice and meat he was eating. I declined, thinking that this was no time to get sick at my stomach. Occasionally, as we sat there, we had faint glimpses of strangers across the runway. The soldiers would raise their rifles, but they didn't fire. I would duck behind the disabled military plane, ready to head into the bush if the shooting started again.

I speculated to myself on what might be happening in Georgetown and Washington. If the small plane and our cowardly pilots had made it back to Georgetown, surely they would have made sure that someone knew what had happened here. But if that was the case, why hadn't a relief plane shown up? I also began to worry that our Embassy in Georgetown might have gotten a garbled message, and passed it on to Washington, where a misleading statement might be issued. They might release an incomplete or incorrect casualty list, in which case my family, friends, and colleagues at *The Post* wouldn't know whether I was alive or dead. It would be a long night for them—as long as the night we faced.

Dwyer got back from the Rum House with Bob Flick and said Javers and I should go up there and join the others. They needed someone to take charge of the defectors and the two Concerned Relatives who were still around, Beverly Oliver, a kindly black woman with two sons at Jonestown, and Carol Boyd, a young white woman with two nieces in the commune. Oliver and Boyd were unharmed. Jim Cobb, another of the Concerned

Relatives, had fled into the bush and Anthony Katsaris was on the floor of the tent, badly wounded.

We walked over to the bar. Our group was crammed into a back bedroom off the kitchen. The lights were out. Some of the survivors were bunched up in clumps in the corners of the room. Others were lying on a bed in a small bedroom nearby.

Javers, Tim Reiterman, and I took up positions around the kitchen table as a ragtag line of defense. We kept the others in the two rooms in the rear and talked to the local police who came in from time to time.

We were told that there were two guards outside the Rum House, one with a gun, the other with a machete. Townspeople were also milling around outside. Mike, the owner of the discotheque we had slept in the night before, was in the Rum House barroom—asleep. He had told us he was afraid to stay in his own house that night because the Jonestown gunmen might think we were there and attack.

The owner's wife at the Rum House fixed us coffee and gave us soft drinks. For food, she produced bananas which were quickly eaten. One of the local policemen showed up to talk with us. He was drunk and started ranting about how he was going to Jonestown to kill everybody there. We tried to calm him down, fearing that in his zeal he might decide to kill us.

I was convinced now that it would be a miracle if we made it through the night. These Guyanese were unreliable. They would be no match, even if they had the taste for it, for the Jonestown kill squad with its automatic weapons. The drunkenness of the guards did nothing to ease my fears.

In a sense, our situation was comical, but I didn't dwell on that. I was exhausted. Between the tension and the drunk locals, I couldn't deal with it anymore. I decided to lie down on the bed beside Mrs. Oliver and try to sleep. We were trapped and if we were attacked again there was nothing we could do.

I slept soundly for a couple of hours and at about 2:30 A.M. got up and went into the kitchen. It was now Sunday, November 19.

Javers and Reiterman were sitting at the kitchen table. We decided to make a list of those who had died, those who had been badly injured, those who had been slightly wounded, and those who had escaped unharmed.

We didn't know the names of most of the defectors, but we also knew that if we got out of this alive and filed our stories, our editors would be unforgiving if we didn't have the names, ages, and serial numbers of everybody involved.

We counted up:

DEAD: Rep. Leo J. Ryan; Don Harris and Bob Brown of NBC; Greg Robinson, the *San Francisco Examiner* photographer. We asked the Jonestown defectors for the name of the fifth dead person. "That's my mother," said Dale Parks. "Patricia Parks." I mumbled: "I'm sorry."

WOUNDED BADLY: Jackie Speier, the Congressman's legislative assistant; Steve Sung, the other NBC camera technician; Anthony Katsaris, one of the Concerned Relatives; Monica Bagby and Vernon Gosney, defectors from Jonestown who had been shot in the little plane.

WOUNDED: Dick Dwyer, deputy chief of mission at the U.S. Embassy in Georgetown; Ron Javers of the *Chronicle,* shot in the shoulder; Tim Reiterman of the *Examiner,* shot in the arm; Beverly Oliver, a Concerned Relative, shot in the foot; and me, only slightly shot in the hip.

MISSING: Jim Cobb, a warm and likable former member of the Temple whose whole family was at Jonestown, Tom Bogue, Chris O'Neill, Tina Turner, Tracy and Brenda Parks, all of whom had fled into the rain forest. We didn't know if they were alive or dead.

Harold Gordell, one of the Jonestown defectors who was with us in the Rum House and who had already boarded the big plane when the shooting started, identified at least three of the gunmen for us. Tom Kice, Sr., had fired an automatic pistol, a .45. Albert Touchette and Joe Wilson fired what looked like M-16s, Gordell said. Stanley Gieg, a young blond chap who usually drove us when we were in the dump truck, had been driving the tractor, but had not fired at anyone, according to Gordell.

The defectors also started opening up about their lives at Jonestown. They told us that they were usually given only rice and some vegetables to eat three times a day. They told us about the black box used to punish people and about the Extra-Care unit where troublemakers or people who attempted to leave Jonestown were taken and placed on heavy sedation for days at a time.

Dale Parks told us about the practice suicide drills Jones had insisted on and a little about his idea of "revolutionary suicide" should Jones's imagined enemies, the CIA and the FBI, attempt to invade the commune in the heart of Guyana.

The horror of what had been going on at Jonestown was now being told by people who had been there. The Concerned Relatives had been right. It was a concentration camp of sorts, but Parks said that many of those who lived there, despite their fear and the long hours they were forced to work, really did not want to leave. Jones had convinced them they would be tortured or killed if they ever went back to the United States.

It was Parks who also told us we had been lucky. He said that if the Jonestown basketball team had not been in Georgetown for a game Friday night, we would all be dead. The basketball team was made up of sharpshooters, the ones trained to kill. We had been attacked by the second string, Parks said, although Tom Kice, Sr., a tall, mean-looking white man with a crew cut whose face I will never forget, was one of the best shots at Jonestown. He was just too old to play basketball.

As we sat there, I decided to start writing. If we got out alive, there would be work to do for *The Post* and I was afraid I might be exhausted when I finally got back to Georgetown. I started with a news story about the massacre itself but then decided I would need a re-write man in Washington to take the information I had and put it together into a story. *The Post* usually doesn't go in for first-person accounts by reporters of what they have been through. But I thought the editors might make an exception this time. They would have to. Unfortunately, I hadn't seen everything that had happened to the others and neither, really, had anyone else.

Writing in longhand with a borrowed pen, I sat at the kitchen table. "PORT KAITUMA, Guyana," I wrote, "dash, dash, dash.

"When the Jonestown truck and tractor suddenly pulled to the side of the small landing strip here, those who knew Peoples Temple best, the 16 disaffected former members, said there was going to be trouble.

"I remember several newsmen, including myself, saying 'no,' these Jonestown people are all so paranoid and crazy that nothing would happen. Yet, a certain urgency developed as Cong. Leo J. Ryan, his aide, Jackie Speier, and Richard Dwyer, the deputy chief of mission at the US Embassy in Georgetown, Guyana's capital, attempted to get the two chartered planes ready and loaded.

"Suddenly, at least three of the men from the Jonestown vehicles began coming toward us. They didn't appear to be armed and I remember thinking that there might be a fistfight or maybe they were coming to try to talk some of the Temple people out of leaving.

"Then, the shooting began. It seemed to be coming from the left side of the aircraft I was standing near, a Guyana airways twin Otter. I ran around the other side and dove behind a wheel, thinking it would protect me.

"Others, I couldn't see exactly whom, were already there and at least two people jumped on top of me as the shooting intensified.

"I lay there, still, hoping they would think I was dead. Shots were being fired very close by. I felt the dirt spraying over me as the bullets came...Suddenly, my left hip burned and I knew I had been hit.

"I remember thinking this is crazy. It can't be happening. I also remember thinking that they were so close it was just a matter of time before I was really hit. I was helpless. I was going to die in the middle of Guyana at the end of one of the most absurd weeks of my life. All I could think about was Thanksgiving...

"The shots that had seemed so close began to seem farther away. I opened my eyes and peered down the runway. I saw the tractor and the truck heading away.

"I jumped up and ran around to the plane's door on the other side. The pilot had revved the engines and, if he was leaving, I wanted to be with him..."

As I was writing, the guards would come in to tell us things. They kept assuring us that the Guyanese Army was on its way. At one point, they told us they had been ordered to collect lanterns to light the airstrip so that a plane could land in the night. At another time, someone came to tell us that there were reports that Jim Jones had carried out his threat, that there had been a mass suicide at Jonestown. The defectors with us told us they were sure that was true, that Jones had been serious when he talked about defending Jonestown to the death.

But they also told us that Jones had said that if he ever ordered "revolutionary suicide," some of his Jonestown marksmen would not be included. Their job, he had said, would be to return to the United States to kill enemies of the Peoples Temple.

Anyone who had defected or written critical articles about Jones was considered enemy number one. The defectors were petrified. Even though I had yet to write a printed word about Jones and his flock, I was scared. At that moment, to be very sure, my lot was very much with the defectors among us.

The most terrifying moment of the night was yet to come. About 4:30 A.M., when it was still pitch black, we heard a motor outside and then what sounded like a shot. The defectors cowered in the corners of their room. I ran into another little bedroom where the Rum House owner and his family were sleeping. I hid behind their bed, sure that gunmen were going to blast away within seconds. My heart was pounding, my thoughts confused. Where the hell was the army? Why hadn't those bastards come? Did anyone know where we were? I had survived the initial attack only to be shot to death in this crappy little bar. This wasn't what I had imagined for myself, dying so far away from home in the company of a bunch of crazies who had left California for the jungle.

After a while, the Rum House owner ventured out into the barroom and came back saying that everything was OK. The noise we had heard had not been a shot, merely a branch or something that had hit the roof. I still don't know about that, but the Jonestown gunmen never returned.

As daylight came over Port Kaituma at about 6 A.M., we received word that the first troops had arrived and were at the airstrip. They had landed the night before at Mathews Ridge, about 30 miles away, and proceeded by train to within three miles of Port Kaituma. They had marched the rest of the way.

Dwyer returned to assure us that the airstrip was now secure. He wanted the survivors to stay at the Rum House because there might still be snipers lurking in the dense vegetation that separated the houses near the strip. I said I wanted to go back with him to the army tent and it was agreed that I would serve as the pool reporter for the other two reporters, who were wounded, to watch the troops take their positions.

I walked over to the tent and looked inside. The wounded, Jackie, Steve, Anthony, and Vernon, had all made it through the night. Bugs were crawling over them and the tent had begun to smell. It had been uncomfortable and, I'm sure, frightening. But they had made it. I couldn't help thinking that if the bullet that had grazed my hip had been aimed an inch or two to the right, I would have spent the night with the badly wounded. Or I would have been left lying with the others near the plane. Dead.

It was now about 7 A.M., Sunday. About 20 soldiers armed with machine guns had taken up positions around the edge of the airstrip. About 80 more armed men were on their way. The first rescue plane did not arrive until about 10:30 A.M.—fully four-and-a-half hours after daybreak. When it came, it was too small to take all the wounded. A medic was on board but he brought no medicine with him. Just aspirins.

At about 11 A.M., the second plane landed. It was a larger, twin Otter like the one disabled halfway down the runway. I had been down there once when the Guyanese insisted that an American be present as they searched the five dead bodies for valuables. Dwyer and I went with them but when we got there, I simply couldn't watch as the bodies were picked over. Dwyer stood off at a distance and kept telling the Guyanese to "get on with it."

Dwyer kept the Congressman's watch and wallet. He gave me Don Harris's and Bob Brown's personal effects to take down to Bob Flick, who was at the tent. When I gave him two wallets and jewelry belonging to his two colleagues, Bob Flick sat down and cried.

We got most of the wounded aboard the smaller military plane and it took off for Georgetown. The larger plane was ready to go but the Jonestown defectors back at the Rum House were refusing to go with it. Their kids were still missing in the jungle and they said the sharpshooters at the Peoples Temple house in Georgetown had a plan to shoot down the rescue planes. Dwyer tried to convince them that Timehri Airport was secured by Guyanese troops—which Dwyer was told but which turned out not to be true. In any case, the rest of us were impatient to finally get out of Port Kaituma. But the Jonestown defectors could not be persuaded to leave.

About noon, on Sunday, Nov. 19, the Guyanese Airways twin Otter carrying me, Bob Flick, Tim Reiterman, Ron Javers, Neville Annibourne of the Guyanese government and Vernon Gosney, the wounded defector, lifted off from the airstrip—fully 17 hours after the massacre. I took one last look at the disabled plane and the five bodies around it. I never thought I would be back.

We landed an hour later at Georgetown. A huge, U.S. air force medivac plane was sitting there waiting for us. The smaller plane had already landed and the badly wounded were already receiving medical attention.

Ron Javers and Tim Reiterman decided they would fly back to the United States on the medivac plane. I went over and had a nurse look at my wound. I decided to stay and file my story from Georgetown.

The military police at the airport insisted that I give them a statement. They put me aboard a waiting Guyanese military helicopter and we headed for the center of Georgetown. I asked if the Peoples Temple house in Georgetown, where the sharpshooting basketball team was located, had been secured. The helicopter pilot overflew the house to show that it was surrounded by troops.

After I gave a brief account of what had happened, the police drove me to the Tower Hotel, where I was staying. I hadn't shaved nor had a shower in two days. I hadn't eaten, except for some bananas, for 27 hours. It was about 3 P.M.

It occurred to me as we drove to the hotel that I still didn't really know whether *The Post* knew all that had happened and I wasn't sure how big a story it all was. Congressmen are a dime a dozen in Washington. They aren't often ambushed in the jungle, but they aren't Senators either. I debated whether I should send a cable explaining all that had happened, suggesting that I thought it was unusual enough to warrant both a news story and a first-person account. Sunday is a slow news day and I thought—or at least I hoped—Washington would be sufficiently interested.

I walked into the lobby of the hotel and no one was there except for the desk clerk and the telephone operator. She looked at me, covered with mud, two days worth of growth on my face, and appeared startled. "Three twelve, please," I said. Then, she knew who I was. "Oh, Mr. Krause, we were praying for you. Your office just called. They've been calling since early this morning."

Well, at least I knew they had an idea of what had happened. They knew I had gone with the Congressman. I still didn't know whether they knew if I was alive or dead. I decided the quickest way to reach Washington was by telex because it often took half an hour or more to get a call through. I wrote out a message and asked the clerk to send it. I went up to my room to take a shower. I returned about 10 minutes later to see if the message had been sent. It had and the clerk gave me a copy:

"19153—PROFOREIGN, EXKRAUSE, PRODESK. JUST GOT BACK EYEM OK. PLS CALL IMMEDIATELY WANT TO GIVE MAIN STORY TO SOMEONE THERE TO WRITE. PROPOSE TO WRITE TWO SIDEBARS. FIRST PERSON OF THE MASSACRE AND ACCOUNT OF A TERRIFYING NIGHT IN THE MIDDLE OF NOWHERE WITH NO PROTECTION TO SPEAK OF. BEST, CHUCK."

Within minutes, Peter Osnos, the *Post*'s foreign editor, and Howard Simons, the paper's managing editor, were on the phone, asking me if I was O.K., telling me they had been up all night as the reports of what had happened were coming in, telling me they had been in constant touch with my family.

I had scared the shit out of them, they told me, and it was awfully good, they said, that I was alive. "And you've got a hell of a story," Osnos told me. Karen DeYoung, who covers Central America and the Caribbean for *The Post*; Len Downie, soon to be *The Post*'s correspondent in London; and Frank Johnston, one of *The Post*'s very best photographers, were on their way by chartered jet. They would be there soon, Osnos said. That was the tip-off. This was a big story and the biggest part was yet to come. I had heard rumors while still in Port Kaituma that Jones and his followers had all killed themselves.

But those rumors were still unconfirmed.

I was still in a towel when Karen, Len, and Frank arrived, about 6:30 P.M. Sunday, Nov. 19. I was dictating my first-person account of the massacre. They hugged me and listened to me read my report of what had happened. They listened as I recounted how close I had come to being killed.

It was only afterward that Len and Karen explained that when they left Washington that morning at 2 A.M. they didn't yet know if I was alive, wounded, or dead. It was only then that I figured out why Len was along. His job was to ship me home—one way or another.

11.

CULTS:
The Battle for the Mind

In an age in which everything was permitted, yet little seemed real, the Reverend Jim Jones promised a refuge.

At his Peoples Temples in California and in the jungles of Guyana, little enough was permitted—disciples surrendered property, privacy, logic, freedoms. And in a blaze of certainty lit by Jones's charisma, paranoia, deceits, and power lust, they found the final reality—death.

"They were smiling...they were genuinely happy," said Mark Lane, a lawyer for the cult who fled into the jungle just before the mass suicide began with the pouring of cyanide into babies' mouths.

Literate, adult Americans, supposedly immunized against such madness by 20th century education and science—these children of the Enlightenment—watched their own children, their spouses, and friends die in foaming convulsions, then waited—even happily—to fall dead in their turns. Only they could understand whatever message they tried to send with their deaths, so it died with them. But they were already long past appreciating this savage paradox.

Genuinely happy. If Lane is right, here lies the real terror for the rest of us.

All week, in the aftermath, historians groped for precedents, psychiatrists for motivations, community leaders for courses of action. How could this have happened? Could it happen again?

Except for the smugness of hindsights offered by foes of the mind-control cults that have emerged in the last decade, there are no simple answers. Instead, a variety of explanations rises out of fact and theory. None suffices in itself. But taken together, they begin to show how the madness of one man could converge with the spirit of an age in upheaval to weave a doomed nexus out of strands ranging from the most ancient of human instincts and customs to the physiology of the mammalian brain.

The comfort, here, is cold indeed. For all that it was bizarre beyond thinking, we don't need a Jim Jones to invoke the supernatural to explain the immolation in Guyana. It was a human—frighteningly human—experience.

It has happened before. Scientists and historians rushed to sweep the carnage into the corner of anomaly, but suicides—even mass suicides—for gods and principles, right and wrong, have occurred in various contexts throughout history.

On April 15, A.D. 73, nearly 1,000 Jewish defenders of the fortress Masada killed themselves rather than be taken prisoner by the besieging Romans. According to Gibbon, the 4th and 5th centuries were marked by the willful martyrdoms of the Donatists, who in seeking heaven "frequently stopped travelers on the public highways and obliged them to inflict the stroke of martyrdom by promise of a reward, if they consented— and by the threat of instant death, if they refused to grant so very singular a favor."

In the 13th century, the fervor of the Albigensians and Cathars (heretical sects in southern France) to avoid the material and seek the spiritual led to numerous deaths from self-willed starvation. A. Alvarez, author of *The*

Savage God, writes that after the conquest of the New World, "treatment at the hands of the Spanish was so cruel that the Indians killed themselves by the thousands rather than endure it . . . In the West Indies, according to the Spanish historian Girolamo Benzoni, four thousand men and countless women and children died by jumping from cliffs or by killing each other."

In the upheavals of the Industrial Revolution, the romantic rebellion turned suicide into a fad. After the appearance of Goethe's novel, *The Sorrows of Young Werther*, Europe was swept by Werther-like suicides. Before the end of World War II, thousands of Japanese soldiers and civilians killed themselves en masse after island battles rather than be dishonored by defeat or surrender. Vietnamese Buddhists registered political protests by setting themselves afire in the 1960s. In 1970, about a dozen French students killed themselves as a political gesture.

But these acts, however irrational, come within the pale of understanding. What promise of heaven, or threat of disaster or dishonor, could have tempted the Peoples Temple disciples?

There were no mercenaries, of course. There was little "situation" to become hopeless. The Peoples Temple was hardly known outside California, much less under attack, except for some West Coast media probes. Jones had sizable political clout—he was head of the San Francisco Housing Authority—and a treasury that may have held millions of dollars. He and his followers had everything, by conventional wisdom, to live for.

But conventional American wisdom has never come to terms with the spiritual upheavals and cult phenomena that started growing out of the disarray of American society a decade ago. As a secular society, we've ignored the power of messianic personalities and their persuasive techniques; and we've forgotten the terrible charm of absolutism—or paranoia—in an age of uncertainty.

"What you have to remember is that leaders like Jones always believe in what they're doing—it's a divine calling," says Syracuse University anthropologist Age-

hananda Bharati. "Once a person is embarked on this
path, it will lead to a power quest. What increases the
power is the dependence of followers. There's a point of
no return, a snapping point. Suddenly you need more and
more power to be sure of yourself—and the quest
becomes linked to the divine calling.

"There are cults and cult leaders all over the world, and
always have been. In the South Pacific we have the cargo
cults [whose members believe in the imminent arrival of
shiploads of goods and money, if they can only have
complete faith that it will happen]. In India there are
gurus such as Sai Baba, who has 10 million followers. But
often, in other cults, something comes along to slow the
momentum of the power quest. People object, for
instance. Jones managed to escape that by taking his
followers to Guyana where there was no media, no
possibility of dissent or investigation."

The divine calling. Like most messiahs and prophets,
Jones, a minister by profession, seems to have started
with a vision. Around 1961 he saw a holocaust consuming
Indianapolis, where he was living. (In *The Varieties of
Religious Experience*, William James writes of "the
psychopathic temperament in religious biography . . . The
subjects here actually feel themselves played upon by
powers beyond their will.") A few years later, in the
archetypal pattern outlined by sociologist Max Weber,
Jones had gathered a group of followers and led them to a
new land in Ukiah, California. He established a
multiracial community which quickly became a political
force in Mendocino County. In 1971 he bought his Geary
Street temple in San Francisco, then expanded to Los
Angeles. He preached socialism and practiced faith
healing, praised Huey Newton and Angela Davis, and
expanded his apocalyptic vision by predicting a fascist
takeover of America.

Being so sure of his ends, Jones had no doubt about
means, a philosophy he passed along to disciples.

According to cult defectors, Jones gained an estimated
following of 20,000 by staging faith healings. As in all

hermetic sects, there were levels of understanding. Those who suspected fraud justified it on the ground that it brought more recruits to the truth of Jim Jones. Jones claimed to be the inheritor of the spirit of Lenin, Jesus, Buddha and the brotherhood of man, to be God, some defectors recall. His means were beyond question.

Jones's paranoia, power and manipulation fed on themselves. His delusions, legitimized by his divine calling, had nothing to check them when he secluded his mission in the Guyana rain forest.

"This wouldn't have happened if they hadn't been so isolated," says Dr. J. Thomas Ungerleider of the UCLA Neuropsychiatric Institute. "With no feedback from the outside world you can do incredible things with peer pressure. Paranoia becomes a useful tool. It's a binding force. With it, you'll engage in peer-pressure activities even more."

And with paranoia, Jones' beliefs that vast conspiracies were arrayed against him only bolstered the certainty of the rightness of his cause, his delusions of importance, and his fears of losing it.

In fact, he may have been courting disaster all the time. "These people look desperately for martyrdom," says Bharati.

"He was irate at the light in which he had been portrayed in the media," Deborah Layton Blakey testified last June. "He felt that as a consequence of having been ridiculed and maligned, he would be denied a place in history. His obsession with his place in history. When pondering the loss of what he considered his rightful place in history, he would grow despondent and say that all was lost."

He made his first mass suicide threat in September 1977, threatening the deaths of all his followers in a mere dispute over a custody case involving one child. The Guyana courts backed off.

Just when it appeared that Representative Leo Ryan would end his investigative mission to Jonestown with a relatively favorable impression, a knifing attempt and then the airfield attack ensured doom. Finally, Jones had vindicated himself by fulfilling his own holocaustic prophecies. He had no choice. His only way out was martyrdom, the more spectacular the better. He had organized it well in advance, so that his followers would die too, arms linked, fallen in embraces, testimony to his wisdom.

It may be that as the cult phenomenon is receding, the cults get a sense of desperation, a sense of need for still more desperate acts," says Yale psychiatrist Robert Jay Lifton, author of *Thought Reform and the Psychology of Totalism.*

Like many of the cults and esoteric religions which began attracting Americans in the late 1960s, Peoples Temple had lost a large part of its membership by 1978. As the upheavals of a decade ago have eased in the somnolent '70s, religious refuges and revelations have lost allure.

It's hard to remember, now, that the turn of the decade was called the third "Great Awakening" by a number of scholars—the first two having been religious revivals in the early 18th and 19th centuries.

Then, as in the late '60s, the nation was swept by proponents of ecstatic religion, in which converts were invited to sense God first-hand, rather than through the intermediaries of theology and sacraments.

The 1960s movement had two stages. In the first, the enemy was not Satan and sin but establishment reason and technology, along with the reality they described. Heroes included British psychiatrist R.D. Laing, who argued in *The Politics of Experience* that schizophrenia was as valid a reality as establishment "sanity." And there was humanist psychologist Abraham Maslow, who advocated the cultivation of the sort of "peak experiences" which mark the lives of saints and prophets.

American spiritual life, often a drab business of church suppers and bingo games, exploded with alternatives: Tibetan Buddhism, the mysterious wisdom of Carlos Castaneda's Don Juan, meditation, glossolalia, primal screaming, biofeedback, and Zen in the art of practically

everything. LSD and other psychedelics became ano-
dynes for the situation once described in graffiti in a
Boston men's room: "Reality is a crutch."

In short, everything became permitted, but reality—
which religion ultimately defines—became very unsure
indeed. The problem was that this movement, rather than
attacking a well-entrenched establishment, was largely a
symptom of its collapse in the storm of Vietnam, racial
strife, generational enmity, and rapidly shifting mores. It
publicly played itself out in Haight-Ashbury, where in
1967 a "summer of love" turned into a nightmare of rape
and drug addiction. Then the Charles Manson murders in
1969 showed that LSD revelations could lead to lethal
paranoia and messianic delusion.

So when the second stage, the so-called mind-control
cults, began to appear with many of the popular esoteric
trappings but none of the chaos, the change was often
greeted with relief.

In the mid-'60s, the Hare Krishna cult arrived in
America. Far from "doing their own thing," cult members
dressed in identical robes, men shaving their heads except
for a top knot. With drums and finger cymbals they
chanted for hours on street corners and harassed
passersby for contributions. Like so many other cult
members, they always looked tired, undernourished and
ecstatic.

In 1968, David "Moses" Berg founded the fire-eyed
Children of God to preach salvation in the face of the
earthquake fever that swept the hip West Coast psyche
that year. In 1971, a 13-year-old Indian named Guru
Maharaj Ji arrived from India to found the Divine Light
Mission. Meanwhile, Sun Myung Moon had come from
Korea to build his Unification Church into the most
controversial of all the cults, which seemed to exist in a
constant barrage of charges ranging from financial
malfeasance to brainwashing.

A host of smaller or less controversial movements
accompanied the cults: Yogi Bhajan's 3HO group (one
cell of which runs the Golden Temple Restaurant),
Transcendental Meditation, and Rev. Jim Jones' Peoples

Temple, among hundreds, perhaps thousands, of groups.

The quest was for certainty. Just as Christians in late antiquity had sought to flee the iron determinism of astrology, these cultists sought an escape from chaos. They tended to stress their identification with middle-class American values, often dressing conservatively.

"The cult promises to provide, and indeed does provide for the convinced convert, the assurance and absolutism the large society so conspicuously lacks," state S. P. Hersh of the National Institute of Mental Health and Ann Macleod of the University of Maryland, in a paper entitled "Cults and Youth Today." "Once the initial decision is taken—to join—the rest comes ready-made: what is right, what is wrong, who shall be saved and who not, how to eat, how to dress, how to live."

The cults represent what anthropologists have long identified in cultures around the world as a revitalization movement, following on what anthropologist Anthony F. C. Wallace calls "a period of cultural distortion," marked by such things as alcoholism, "extreme passivity and indolence, intragroup violence, disregard of kinship and sexual mores, irresponsibility in public officials..."

Examples of such movements include the Plains Indians' Ghost Dance movement in the late 19th century, the Boxer Rebellion in China, the South Seas cargo cults, and even the Bolshevik Revolution of 1917.

As Wallace explains it, a prophet has one or several hallucinatory visions, such as Jones's vision of a holocaust. He preaches his revelations to people "in an evangelistic or messianic spirit." Then "converts are made by the prophet. Some undergo hysterical seizures induced by suggestion in a crowd situation; some experience an ecstatic vision in private circumstances; some are convinced by more or less rational arguments..." The prophet changes his message to fit his needs. "In instances where organized hostility to the movement develops, a crystallization of counter-hostility against unbelievers frequently occurs, and emphasis shifts from cultivation of the ideal to combat against the unbeliever."

●   ●   ●

Such is the fate of a large number of American cults. That combat sometimes takes the form of ridiculously high-stakes gambles: the Children of God predicted the end of the world with the arrival of the comet Kohoutek; Guru Maharaj Ji's adherents rented the Houston Astrodome for a mammoth convention at which they predicted apocalyptic confirmation of their doctrine, even setting aside spaces in the parking lot for flying saucers.

More recently, the Transcendental Meditation movement tried to bolster declining membership with claims that they could teach adherents to levitate and fly.

The combat has taken harsher forms. In the past year, members of Synanon, a California group originally founded in the 1950s to treat drug addiction, have been accused of attempting to murder a prosecutor by putting a rattlesnake in his mailbox. Members of the Church of Scientology, another group dating from the '50s, were indicted for stealing files the government had maintained on the group. One prankster who hit Guru Maharaj Ji in the face with a pie later had his skull fractured with a hammer wielded, he charged, by a Divine Light Mission official. Last summer, a self-styled renegade Mormon prophet named Immanuel David, who had been visited like Jones by holocaustic visions, killed himself. The next morning his wife helped their seven children jump from their eleventh-floor hotel room, then followed them. And Jim Jones abandoned America, hurling back the threats of assassination and suicide that became fact last week.

"The unnatural passivism of [cult] members," is actually "a carefully muted aggressiveness," write Katherine V. Kemp and John R. Lion, professors of psychiatry at the University of Maryland School of Medicine.

The cults have flourished, too, because the American establishment, founded on rationalism and Lockean tabula rasa theories of the mind (in which mankind is seen to be infinitely educable, with no inborn predispositions) is extremely reluctant to admit that human beings may be innately susceptible to certain persuasive techniques. In *Battle for the Mind* and *The Mind Possessed,* British neurologist William Sargant has cited laboratory evidence gathered by Pavlov and his own observations of acute combat stress in World War II as part of a hypothesis that stress, if strong enough, "can produce a marked increase in hysterical suggestibility so that the individual becomes susceptible to influences in his environment to which he was formerly immune." Says anthropologist Bharati, "It can happen to anybody."

Former cult members recite a litany of stress they underwent: sleep deprivation, hunger, constant haranguing, and in the case of Peoples Temple, public beatings and threats of death.

Psychiatrist Lifton notes: "Mind control comes when you have total control of communication in an environment; when you have manipulation inside the group, such as constant self-criticism and confessing; and manipulation of individual guilt."

If Sargant is right, we are innately and physically susceptible. Ethologist Konrad Lorenz brings it into the realm of instinct in *On Aggression.* Once instilled with the sort of paranoia Jones purveyed, the follower is driven by "militant enthusiasm by which any group defends its own social norms and rites against another group not possessing them . . . One is ready to abandon all for the call of what, in the moment of this specific emotion, seems to be a sacred duty."

So lured by security and order, betrayed by physiology and instinct, cult members can be willing to follow their leaders even into death.

Some cult observers maintain that it is largely those who are mentally ill or close to it who join the cults. Dr. John Clark, a professor of psychiatry at the Harvard Medical School, has estimated from his studies that 58 percent of those who join cults are schizophrenic, either chronic or borderline. But he adds that 42 percent of those he examined were neither ill nor damaged.

In any case, we are left with the hideous vision of smiling disciples drinking cyanide. We can explain it away as a terrible accident, saying that the cult members were duped into thinking the exercise was just another rehearsal. We could claim that the cultists were forced to kill themselves. But that does not explain the smiles, the failure of more members to flee, the dying with arms linked with fellow disciples. In fact, a survivor recalls one woman objecting, only to be shouted down with cries of "traitor."

UCLA's Ungerleider speculates that "they may have killed themselves willingly out of what Anna Freud called 'identification with the aggressor.' It's a defense mechanism in hopeless situations, when the ego is overwhelmed. It explains why some Jews would actually help each other into the gas chambers in concentration camps." Even when the dying began, and panic twitched through the camp, Jones could keep the mad momentum going by insisting that they must "die with dignity."

We might do well to consider that they died knowingly, believing that death was beautiful, as Jones kept chanting into his microphone. Indeed, if they shared his paranoia, his vision of the holocaust, the fate that awaited the community after the murder of Representative Ryan was far worse than death.

In the terms of French sociologist Emile Durkheim, they had preached an "altruistic" suicide, for the glory of socialism. But when the time came, it was merely "anomic"—self-destruction in the face of the disintegration of all that was meaningful, a universe which existed only in their minds.

To his followers, Jones was a god whose power they could take into themselves merely by obeying him. It may have seemed, as they drank the cyanide, that for one moment they would share in ultimate power—the power of life and death. If, in the falling and convulsions, that moment ever came, no one will ever know.

12.

SCOOP:
Getting the Story Out

Journalists, by and large, behave badly. The press horde that descended on Georgetown in the week of November 19 was no exception to that axiom. Furthermore, bad behavior tends to become execrable when airports are jammed, hotel rooms are scarce, and phone service is just marginal to the normal needs of a place. Georgetown, with its fragile, gingerbread charm, conformed to all these requirements.

The small Ryan delegation that had arrived the previous week seemed already to have strained the city's public accommodations. But when the locust invasion of world press arrived, things turned to bedlam. They came wheeling out of the sky, poised as always to feed on catastrophe, with their babble of different tongues and surprisingly uniform lines of equipment: Japanese cameras and tape recorders, German or Italian portable typewriters, and ecumenical rudeness in all languages.

Item: two German reporters storming out of the local police station declaiming against the "inefficiency" of the imperturbable Guyanese bureaucracy.

Item: *The New York Times* correspondent proclaiming the influence of his newspaper while demanding an immediate call to New York of an overworked switchboard operator in the Tower Hotel. "Maybe I will, maybe I won't," she muttered after he left.

Item: Television correspondents jumping into a cab with camera and sound men to interview another reporter on his way to the airport.

Item: One veteran Washington newspaper correspondent giving an avuncular warning to a younger colleague about the prostitutes sashaying through a hotel lobby: "Watch it, man. In this town you can get a bad case of clap by just pissing into the wind."

From the United States mainland the only air connections with Guyana were through New York and Miami, routing through Port-of-Spain and other Caribbean capitals with long layovers and transfers. The arrival point was Timehri International Airport, 26 miles from Georgetown. So the task of booking flights to Georgetown from the United States was formidable; from any other part of the globe it was even more so. Inevitably the three free-spending American television networks and affluent newspapers, chartered their own sleek Lear jets. By the time most of world-class journalism arrived in Georgetown, its mood was foul.

The slow-moving ambience of Guyana was bound to make things worse. Novelist V. S. Naipaul caught the spirit of lethargy in an admirable essay on what was then British Guiana.

"Georgetown," he wrote, "most exquisite city in the British Caribbean, is for the visitor the most exasperating. Try getting a cup of coffee in the morning. The thing is impossible. Yesterday you expressed a dislike for lukewarm "instant" coffee, particularly when the coffee is placed on the water and not the water on the coffee; so this morning your hotel offers you half a teaspoonful of last year's coffee grounds in a pint of lukewarm water, since in your folly you said that you 'used' ground coffee—'use,' revealingly, being the Guianese word for 'drink' or 'eat.'

"... When you came down this morning at a-quarter-past-seven and inquired why you had not been awakened at half-past-six, as you had asked, the middle-aged waiter, with a look of terror, said it wasn't half-past six as yet . . ."

Into this world, which had changed little since Naipaul wrote in 1962, came the legions of the press in the Lear jets, with their Nikon cameras and Sony recorders. Despite its having won independence from British rule, the capital retained all the trappings of British colonial bureaucracy under a benign Socialist administration headed by Forbes Burnham, who prefers to be addressed as "comrade." Its population of 780,000 is roughly half East Indian, 40 percent black with a remaining mix of Chinese, indigenous Amerindians, and "white" Guyanese of British descent who stayed after independence in 1966.

One of the first moves of the American news media upon establishing camp in Guyana was to commandeer most of the functioning cabs on a full-time basis, making it necessary for others in the press to share the precarious, winding ride from the airport to town with the local populace on decrepit buses.

The world media descended on six hotels ranging from the correct, stiff-upper-lip British style of the Pegasus along Georgetown's silt-filled ocean front to mattresses on the floors of squalid flop houses. For the press, the most favored hotel was the Tower, which compensated for its peeling paint and falling plaster with a competent cuisine of English, French, and Indian dishes served by Indian waiters brimming over with political and journalistic gossip—but little sound information.

Within the first 24 hours of the great press descent, several reporters had encountered a quaint welcome on the streets of the city. These are described as "choke-and-rob," in which the new visitor has his arm grabbed suddenly from behind or his windpipe given a sharp blow while he is separated from his watch or wallet. Eventually the Guyanese government issued warnings to the press as part of its formal indoctrination to the country. Reporters found themselves taking cabs for half a block between their hotel and their destinations to avoid these costly encounters. One FBI agent, accosted by a choke-and-robber, shot him on the spot, not fatally.

To book a phone call either to Washington or to Guyana in the Tower (which, needless to say, was devoid of a tower), it was necessary to go downstairs to the switchboard, which was manned uniformly by a single operator. It took ten to thirty minutes for calls to get through—and sometimes a comparable number of dollars as inducements.

Evelyn Waugh described the information-gathering process in Guyana with eerie accuracy some four decades ago in *Scoop*, his satirical novel about the British and American press behavior in the mythical central African republic of Ishmaelia. However awful was the reality in the jungle 140 miles to the northwest, the 100-odd journalists confined to Georgetown found themselves in a stew of wild rumor, professional anxiety, and frantic urgings from their home offices to race to the catastrophe. Some reporters were awakened in their hotel rooms in the middle of the night by Australian or New Zealand voices asking for five-minute "beeper" radio interviews on the latest gory details. Others were apprised by their editors of the prospects for "instant" books on the massacre, such as this one, promising substantial advances.

One of the central points of information in Georgetown was the office of Guyanese Minister of Information Shirley Field-Ridley, a bright and attractive black woman who shuttled constantly between Cabinet meetings and press briefings. The Ministry of Information was housed, like most government agencies, in a ramshackle, yellowing structure. The slow-whirling ceiling fans recirculated hot air masses over the chipped and battered furniture, along the peeling walls and over the lethargic bureaucracy waiting to add yet another journalist's name to yet another list.

Naipaul wrote: "The malarial sluggishness of the Guianese is known throughout the Caribbean and is recognized even in British Guiana...I was told that it is dangerous to leave a Guianese in charge of a surveying station in the bush: the surveyor will return to find the hut collapsed, instruments rusted, and the Guianese mad."

Hardly more helpful was the American Embassy

presided over by John Burke, a 53-year-old professional foreign service officer with a taste for Bach and Schubert, with a reputation for unflappability that some suggest may stem from inability to perceive a serious oncoming crisis. His information deputy was Stepney Kibble, a black U.S. career officer for whom Guyana was to be the crowning assignment in a 30-year career. He planned to retire to a plot that he had providentially purchased years earlier in New Mexico. Dutiful as Kibble was in his role as embassy spokesman, he came under attack from certain quarters in the press on varying grounds, chief among them timidity and incompetence.

Kibble would say nothing that had not been cleared by the Embassy. Even after Kibble had been put in charge of the military press room set up on the lobby floor of the United States Information Agency library, he would volunteer no information. Relentlessly, he would refer newsmen to other sources—Minister of Information Field-Ridley or the American military task force spokesman, Air Force Capt. John J. Moscatelli, a stiff, dark-haired and olive-skinned man with a preference for dark-rimmed glasses and a deep aversion to smiling. Moscatelli would bark out to reporters the numbing catalogue of updated body counts, body bags, bodies flown to Timehri, bodies transferred to aluminum cases, bodies flown to Dover, Delaware. If a reporter persisted in questioning Kibble, he would repeat the drumfire of statistics, moving his finger along the text and numbers as he recited.

From television, movies, and romanticized fiction, popular myths have arisen about journalists in trench coats and bush jackets roaming the world as eyewitnesses to history. The Jonestown story, however, demonstrated again the farcical and second-hand nature of what often passes for "news gathering."

Unable to reach the Jonestown settlement or even Port Kaituma 150 miles away, the news locusts in Georgetown resorted to the time-honored practice of interviewing one another, collecting stale stories, and embellishing bureaucratic utterances in such a way as to convey the

impression that "I am there." One reporter, fortunate
enough to fly briefly over the Jones settlement in the
jungle, filed a story with the dateline, "Jonestown,
Guyana." A major newspaper filled its pages for days with
detailed stories on the massacre in Jonestown, though its
reporters were stranded in Georgetown where they had to
rely on second-hand descriptions of the carnage.

And so, for the stranded correspondent in Georgetown
the imperative in life was getting to Jonestown. On
Monday, November 20, Information Minister Field-
Ridley announced at her only press conference that a pool
of three newspersons could accompany Guyanese
authorities by air to Jonestown.

The *Washington Post*'s Krause was sitting in the front
row of reporters and Leonard Downie, Jr., another *Post*
reporter who had just arrived from Washington, was
sitting a few seats away, unrecognized. In the clamor of
voices demanding the coveted seats, Downie's voice rose
above the others. "Why don't you let Krause go? He
deserves it!" Krause's colleagues, still not recognizing
Downie's affiliation, quickly agreed with him in an
uncharacteristic burst of generosity, given the keenness of
the competition. Through quirks of chance and cunning,
the photographer who won the pool seat on the airplane
was Frank Johnston, also of *The Washington Post*. When
Field-Ridley noticed the common affiliation of Krause
and Johnston, she looked up with a smile. Should there be
two people from the same organization, she asked.

Krause was going because he had been a special case,
Downie quickly explained, and Johnston had been
nominated by their peers. "Besides they are already on
their way to the airport," Downie added.

The Post's Downie then turned to his colleagues and
promised them a full pool report.

13.

MONDAY, NOVEMBER 20:
"The babies went first."

From the air, Jonestown looked as if someone had scattered colored paper around the central pavilion—red paper, blue paper, yellow, and green. It looked as if there had been a celebration, a party, that the Reverend Jim Jones had uncharacteristically allowed his followers to enjoy—without forcing them to clean up.

Those were my first thoughts as I returned to Jonestown on Monday, November 20, just 48 hours after I had left for what I thought would surely be the last time.

Now, I was on my way back, by helicopter, to view a sight that would transfix a world inured to war and violence and death. The absolute horror of what lay below, the madness and desperation of the man who ordered it all, and the almost banal way he caused them to die—a potion of grape drink, cyanide and tranquilizers—was almost beyond comprehension.

I am also tempted to say beyond belief. Except that the scraps of what appeared from the air to be paper, were in fact the shorts and shirts, trousers and blouses of more than 900 terrorized, misguided, and ultimately supremely loyal followers of a man gone mad, the Reverend Jim Jones.

There on the ground, as we hovered overhead, were the grisly remains of Jones's last great act of madness. There on the ground were the men, women, and children, white and black, well-educated and untutored, who had believed blindly in the man they called "Father."

There on the ground were the bodies, already beginning to decompose in the tropical heat, of those who had followed Jones to the wilderness. The bodies of those who had, many of them voluntarily, carried out Jones's last twisted vision, the victims of what Father called "revolutionary suicide" and had code-named "White Night."

Once the true dimensions of what had happened were known, newspapers and magazines would set their reporters and researchers to work trying to find historical precedents for this act of mass suicide-murder. Publications throughout the world would recall the self-slaughter of the Jewish defenders of the Masada in A.D. 73, the self-willed starvation of the heretical Albigensian and Cathars sects in the 13th century and the suicides during World War II of Japanese civilians and soldiers in Saipan, who jumped into the sea.

They would look for these precedents out of desperation, trying to reassure themselves and their readers that the Jonestown horror was not entirely a product of our time, of the modern, brutal, alienated society in which we live. I will leave that to others. On Monday, November 20, I was on my way to confront the stark and gruesome reality of what had happened at Jonestown a few hours after the Port Kaituma massacre—an incident that, of itself, was one of the most bizarre acts of recent times.

My thoughts, as the Guyanese military helicopter landed in a field about 300 yards from the pavilion where I had first met Jones three days before, ran to extremes.

As the first reporter allowed into Jonestown to view the carnage, my job demanded that I bring back a detailed account of what had happened and try to find words to describe the horror that I saw.

But, because I was a survivor of the Port Kaituma massacre, there were personal reasons for going back as well. I was hoping not to find the bodies of some of the people I had grown fond of during my short stay at Jonestown, people like Sarah and Richard Tropp, whose unselfish and rational reasons for wanting to create a better world in the rain forests of Guyana had touched me.

And, quite truthfully, I was also going back to see for myself that Jim Jones and the henchmen he had sent to kill me and the others in Representative Leo J. Ryan's party were among the dead. I particularly wanted to find the body of Tom Kice, Sr., the tall, gray-haired man with a crew cut, whose mean, demented expression I will never forget as he crossed the airstrip to kill us. And the body of Stanley Gieg, the young, blond-haired fellow who was driving the tractor when the shooting began.

I had never seen a person shot to death before Saturday afternoon, November 18. But, in the next 48 hours I had, to my own surprise, become largely numb. Five bodies or 500 bodies. What was the difference? The carnage here was far more grotesque than what I had seen at the airstrip. But the revulsion I expected to feel was missing. I had thought I might throw up at the sight of so many bodies lying in their own pools of vomit and blood.

Instead, I felt more like crying. It was all so senseless, so cruel, so tragic. Most of these people lying on the ground before me were innocent, just as innocent as the five people who had died in the burst of gunfire that was the catalyst for Jones to order the end of his world.

As I approached the radio shack near the pavilion, I saw the bodies close up for the first time. There must have been 40 or 50 of them there on the neat lawn in front of the communications center that had been Jonestown's link to Georgetown, San Francisco, and the outside world.

I only recognized one of the bodies, that of a jovial, heavyset white woman who had served me coffee and cheese sandwiches two days before. She had introduced me to her daughter, a pretty girl with long brown hair, and we had laughed together about something I can no longer remember.

Now I saw the mother's body near the radio shack. She was still wearing the gaily-flowered long dress she had worn the last time I saw her alive. She was, like most of the others, lying on her stomach, a clot of dried blood stuck in her right nostril. My God, I thought. Why?

I stared at the clumps of bodies in front of the communications center. I couldn't bring myself to leave them. I noticed that many of them had died with their arms around each other, men and women, white and black, young and old. Little babies were lying on the ground, too. Near their mothers and fathers. Dead.

Finally, I turned back toward the main pavilion and noticed the dogs that lay dead on the sidewalk. The dogs, I thought. What had they done?

Then I realized that Jones had meant to leave nothing, not even the animals, to bear witness to the final horror. There were to be no survivors. Even the dogs and Mr. Muggs, Jonestown's pet chimpanzee, had their place in the long white night into which the Peoples Temple had been ordered by the mad Mr. Jones.

The heat and the stench were overpowering. There was nothing to drink because Jones had ordered the community water supply contaminated with poison. The Guyanese soldiers who guarded Jonestown said that a cache of soft drinks had been found. But they decided, even though the bottles hadn't been opened, that it would be risky to drink them.

C.A. (Skip) Roberts, the assistant police commissioner from Georgetown who was in charge of the Guyanese forces at Jonestown, came along just as I was about to inspect the main pavilion. I had met him the day before when I was taken to the police station immediately after I arrived at Temehri airport. He had insisted that I give him a statement about the Port Kaituma massacre before I returned to my hotel.

I asked Roberts if Jones and his wife, Marceline, were among the dead. Yes, he told me. Marcie was over there by the pavilion. And Jones was lying, shot to death, on the podium that he had used as his altar. Only three of the bodies found so far had died of gunshot wounds, Roberts said. Jones, his mistress, Maria Katsaris, whose brother Anthony had come along with Ryan to try to persuade his sister to leave, and one other, so far unidentified, Temple member.

Roberts said, with both authority and what seemed at the time, precision, that there were 383 bodies scattered around the altar, in the immediate vicinity of the pavilion. Another 21 or 22 bodies had been found elsewhere, he added.

In all, 404 or 405 bodies had been found, Roberts said. It appeared that hundreds of persons known to be living at Jonestown at the time of the suicide-murder rite had either escaped or been killed outside the settlement itself, he said. There was no question of the number of bodies lying around us, he said.

The still half-full tub of poisonous liquid that had served as Jones's agent of death stood over there, Roberts said, pointing a few feet away. The poison was a reddish concoction composed of Flavor Aid, cyanide, and, possibly, tranquilizers and other drugs that had been prepared by the Jonestown doctor, Lawrence Schacht. Schacht was dead, too, Roberts said.

Both Mark Lane and Charles E. Garry, the lawyers we had left behind the Saturday before, had managed to escape. There were, in addition, three known survivors who had been meant to die but had managed to escape during the final confusion.

Then there were others: Mike Prokes, Tim and Mike Carter, whose survival was still unexplained. Prokes and the Carter brothers, who had been among the top leaders at Jonestown, had made their way into Port Kaituma, bringing with them a gun and a suitcase full of money. I told Roberts I thought they were dangerous, and he agreed.

Roberts told me that his men had found more than 800 U.S. passports, indicating that there had been at least that many people living at Jonestown the week before. He said his men had also found an arsenal of weapons, including 40 to 50 automatic rifles, revolvers and other guns, 20 or more bows and arrows "and hundreds of thousands of rounds of ammunition."

We walked over to a table where this arsenal was on display and I couldn't help thinking of Jones's anger when Don Harris had asked him the previous Saturday about the one gun we had learned about. "A bold-faced lie," Jones had thundered. "We are defeated by lies."

The irony of those words rushed into my mind. The lies Jones had been defeated by were obviously his own. Not those of the Concerned Relatives, the press, and the others who had tried to expose the deteriorating situation at Jonestown. It had been, I now understood only too well, the tropical concentration camp its critics said it was—led by a man increasingly consumed by his own dark visions. Tim Stoen had described Jones as "a classic paranoid schizophrenic." At the time, I had thought Stoen was the madman. Now, standing in the midst of the guns and the bodies and the family-sized containers of cyanide that had been found, I knew the truth. If only it had been exposed before all of this, I thought.

In the classroom tent where Roberts was collecting the weapons that were still being found, the ammunition, the bows and arrows, the revolvers and the poisonous drugs, a rather handsome black man, dressed in a tank top T-shirt with a string of beads around his neck, approached.

Roberts suggested I might want to ask him some questions. He had, Roberts said, witnessed much of the denouement of Jonestown before managing to escape with his life. The man's name was Odell Rhodes, 36, who described himself as a former drug addict from Detroit who had joined the Peoples Temple to kick his habit and had stayed on until almost the very end.

Rhodes described for me what had happened the previous Saturday about 5:30 P.M., when the Jonestown gunmen returned from Port Kaituma to report on their deadly mission. They told Jones that Representative Ryan had been killed, along with most of the newsmen, but that some had survived.

Jones, Rhodes said, immediately called his followers, using the loud speaker system strung up throughout the commune, to a meeting at the pavilion. "Alert, alert, alert," Jones had screamed, ordering everyone to the meeting that was to be their last.

"He told us that we've shot the Senator," Rhodes recalled. "You know there's going to be trouble, he said." The time had come to commit the mass, revolutionary suicide his faithful had practiced several times before.

Armed guards took positions around the pavilion to insure that no one tried to escape. Dr. Schacht and his medical team brought the vat and began mixing the grape-flavored liquid that would soon be squirted into the mouths of infants and children and poured down the throats of teenagers and adults.

Meanwhile, Rhodes said, Jones remained in the pavilion, watching over the preparations, exhorting his followers to die with dignity and explaining his original plan to make sure that Congressman Ryan never reached Georgetown and the United States.

Larry Layton, Rhodes said, had been selected to

pretend that he was a defector and to accompany the Ryan party to the airstrip. The plan was that he would get a seat aboard the Congressman's plane and then, once it was airborne, shoot the pilot and co-pilot so that the plane would crash in the dense, almost impenetrable rain forest. A team of other gunmen had been sent along in the Jonestown tractor to finish off any members of the Ryan party who might remain behind.

Layton boarded the wrong plane, however, and was only able to shoot two of those aboard before his gun jammed. The extra gunmen then tried to kill the rest of the party that had either boarded or were near the larger plane. For some unknown reason, they left before killing everyone and returned to report their partial failure.

"When the truck came back, he said, 'It's too late, we've all got to kill ourselves,'" Rhodes said. "One woman, Christine Miller, protested, but the crowd started shouting her down."

Jones continued his wild exhortations, explaining that Jonestown would soon be surrounded by enemy forces, that the only dignity for those who had come this far was death. The potion was ready now and a young mother approached the vat and watched as the doctor took a syringe filled with grape-flavored cyanide and squirted it down the throat of her young child.

"They started with the babies," Rhodes told me, the horror of it all still fresh in his mind, his eyes, his voice. I scribbled his words into my notebook and suddenly felt nauseous.

Some of the "faithful" made feeble attempts to escape, but were turned back by the guards. At one point, an old man who resisted taking the poison was held down while the liquid was forcibly poured down his throat. "It just got all out of order. Babies were screaming, children were screaming." Rhodes recalled softly, remembering the scene during which Jones kept exhorting his flock to die with dignity.

Rhodes estimated that it took four to five minutes for the deadly liquid to take its final effect. People would step up into line, drink the potion and then join other family members to wait for the end.

They would gasp for breath, their eyes would roll upward and then they would go into convulsions. They would vomit, shudder, and die. Rhodes watched the horror unfolding before his eyes. He had no real hope of escaping until Dr. Schacht said he needed a stethoscope. Rhodes said he eagerly volunteered to go with one of the nurses to fetch one.

He walked with her through the armed guards, who let him pass. When the nurse went into Schacht's office, Rhodes said he quickly bolted and hid under a building until about 7 P.M. Saturday, when the grisly ritual seemed to be over.

He said he walked as fast as he could to Port Kaituma, hoping to alert the police there to what had happened. He said he hoped they might be able to get to Jonestown to save some of those who might have escaped or might somehow have survived the poison. The first Guyanese troops did not reach Jonestown until late Sunday, but Roberts told me that it was Rhodes's initial report Saturday night that had provided the first indication that Jones had carried through with his last, twisted vision.

I asked Roberts if Tom Kice's body had been found. He told me that it had not, lending more credence to the theory that the approximately 500 Jonestown residents who had not yet been found might have been marched off to be shot in the rain forest. Mark Lane and Charles Garry said they had heard a volley of gunshots as they were leaving Jonestown, lending more support to the theory.

It was not until three days later that U.S. military teams brought into Jonestown to remove the bodies would discover that the Guyanese count was very wrong. Under the bodies we saw were other bodies and, in some cases, more bodies under those.

The stench and the way the bodies were spread

out near the pavilion, coupled with the precise numbers Roberts offered Monday, made it difficult and seemingly unnecessary to count the bodies myself.

I walked from the schoolroom tent where I had talked with Roberts and Rhodes toward the pavilion. I wanted to see Marceline and Jim. She was lying on her back, less than five feet from the vat of poison. He was lying, his fat stomach protruding upward, his shirt pulled halfway off his chest, on the altar. Blood covered his face. Good, I thought. He is, in fact, dead.

I walked to the other side of the pavilion, not far from where Representative Ryan had first alerted me to the oddity of all of the older people standing and jiving to the soul music that had been played in this very place the Friday night before. I wanted to see Stanley Gieg's body, just to make sure. His face was already grayish-blue, but there was no doubt in my mind that what I saw was his corpse.

I walked back to look at the altar again. It was littered with bodies, most of them probably Temple leaders, who had had the honor of dying next to Father. On the steps leading to the altar was a young black boy, who had died genuflecting before the demented man these people thought of as their god.

I had had enough. There were only two things more I wanted to do. I wanted to see the body of Sarah Tropp, whom I had kissed as I left Jonestown the last time and for whom I felt an unexplained fondness, and the body of Maria Katsaris, whose brother had cried as he left her to her fate.

Sarah lay all alone, apart from the others, not far from the pavilion. She was on her stomach, her short hair, now filthy and overrun with bugs, clinging to her head. I was truly sorry. I never found her brother, Richard.

I then walked down to Jones's house, where I had never been before. It had not been part of the tour. Frank Johnston, *The Post* photographer, came with me, but decided, when he saw the place, that he had enough pictures. I couldn't blame him. We had seen enough bodies and had captured, both in our minds and, in his case on film, the horror of the final desperate hour at Jonestown.

But I had an odd compulsion to see Maria Katsaris's body, not because I had felt in any way close to her, but because I thought I should see it so that I could tell Anthony and his father, Steve, that there was no doubt that she had died. With more than 400 Jonestown residents unaccounted for, I knew they would still be hoping that somehow she had escaped. I didn't want to be the bearer of bad news, but I thought it would be better to be able to tell them that I had seen her body than to leave them wondering for days or weeks . . . or possibly forever.

Maria's body lay on a bed in Jim Jones's house. There was no question that it was she. Roberts told me she had been shot rather than poisoned, but I couldn't see where the bullet had entered her body. But there was no question that Maria Katsaris had died along with her lover, the Reverend Jim Jones.

I returned to a warehouse away from the pavilion where Rhodes and his men were gathered. The trunk filled with U.S. passports was there and Frank took some pictures. I asked Roberts if he had discovered much money and he smiled. "Substantial amounts," he said. "What does that mean?" I asked.

The game went on for a minute or two, but finally we both tired of it. The sun was hot, there was nothing to eat or drink, and the horror was starting to take its effect. He said I wouldn't be wrong if I reported that so far more than half a million dollars in cash had been located and that more was being discovered. Wallets full of Social Security checks had been found, as well as gold, diamonds, and jewelry. In all, Rhodes estimated more than $1.5 million worth of readily negotiable checks, currency, and precious metals had been discovered.

That explained, among other things, why, despite

their pleas of poverty, Jones had had no trouble coming up with 5,000 Guyanese dollars the Saturday before to help pay for the defectors to return to the United States.

We had been at Jonestown for almost an hour-and-a-half when the helicopter finally returned to take us back to the Port Kaituma airstrip. Our crippled twin Otter aircraft was exactly where it had been when the attack on Congressman Ryan and the rest of us began.

Shortly after 7 P.M., Monday, November 20, we headed back to Georgetown; the horror of what I had seen was etched permanently in my mind.

In the days ahead, some of the unfinished parts of the story would fall into place. Others might never be finished.

Larry Layton, who had tried to kill some of us at the airstrip, was in police custody in Georgetown. Linda Sharon Amos, who had been at the airport when I arrived in Guyana, was dead in the Temple's Georgetown house. Her throat and the throats of her three children were slashed. John-John Stoen, whom Tim and Grace Stoen had come to bring home, was dead at Jonestown. Mike Prokes, Mike and Tim Carter, three of Jim Jones's most loyal lieutenants, survived the holocaust at Jonestown and soon showed up in Georgetown with large sums of cash. They had carried away from the Temple a suitcase loaded with money.

Richard Dwyer, Jackie Speier, Tim Reiterman, Ron Javers, Anthony Katsaris, Steve Sung, and Vernon Gosney had been hospitalized to repair the wounds they received during the attack at the airstrip two days before. Physically, they would all recover. But, in another way, all of us would carry away from Guyana wounds that might never heal.

For myself, I'll carry around for a long time—maybe forever—the memory of the terror we all felt when the Jonestown gunmen fired at us that muggy day at the airstrip. And I'll carry around a scar from a small wound in my hip.

More importantly, I'll always wonder why I was spared when so many around me at Port Kaituma were shot to death at point-blank range—Congressman Leo J. Ryan, Don Harris, Bob Brown, Greg Robinson, and Mrs. Parks. At Jonestown, it was pretty obvious that I was sympathetic to the social experiment going on there and thought has crossed my mind that maybe Sarah or Richard Tropp asked that I not be killed. Or, maybe, the gunmen simply overlooked me. I'm certain I'll never know the answer to that life or death question.

As a reporter, I wonder now if I was terribly naive at Jonestown. Did I ignore evidence that Jonestown was closer to what the Concerned Relatives said it was—a concentration camp run by a mad man—than the tropical paradise Jones and the others claimed. But that question is still not settled in my mind. Even now, I am not convinced that the majority of people there wanted to leave, no matter what the reality of Jonestown.

Whether the Jonestown holocaust has any meaning beyond the event itself is a question I'll leave to others for now.

I have more immediate concerns. What happens for example, to Jim Jones's lieutenants who escaped with guns and money from the Temple on the White Night? Are they going to seek revenge on their critics? Or on me?

That thought hit me hard while writing this book. The news reports of the murders of San Francisco Mayor George Moscone and City Supervisor Harvey Milk immediately put into my mind the fear that they had been killed by followers of Jones. That was wrong, but the fear remains.

Whatever happens, I suppose my life, to some extent, is bound to Jim Jones and his Peoples Temple in ways that I could never have imagined when I first arrived in Guyana.

Like so many others, this awful man will be with me until I die.

14.

BODY COUNT:
End of the White Night

The myths, mysteries, and primitive fears that surrounded the Peoples Temple in life, surrounded it in death. By one account, Jim Jones, the cult's Father, had escaped the holocaust at Jonestown and was headed for the United States with a squad of assassins to take revenge on his critics. Another story had lieutenants of Jones making their way out of the jungle with strongboxes of gold and diamonds and suitcases of money destined for the Soviet Embassy in Georgetown, Guyana. There was yet another report of a search at the jungle Temple for a $3 million treasure hidden somewhere in Jonestown.

The greatest mystery, however, turned on the whereabouts of anywhere from 300 to 800 cult members who were believed to have disobeyed or rebelled at the mass suicide order given by Jim Jones on Saturday, November 19. Two days earlier, Jones and one of his lawyers, the ubiquitous Mark Lane, told Congressman Leo Ryan and other members of the investigating group that visited Jonestown, that the community consisted of 1,200 people. Reporters in the group were skeptical of that number and came up with their own estimate of 800

to 1,000. The U.S. State Department would later report
that more than 800 passports were found at Jonestown
after the suicide rite.

It was these numbers that fueled the mystery of
Jonestown, beginning on Monday, November 20. That
morning, the Guyanese Minister of Information, Shirley
Field-Ridley, announced to the horde of journalists
assembling in Georgetown that Guyanese troops had
reached Jonestown the previous night. They had
discovered, she said, a scene of indescribable horror at the
jungle Temple. In the great pavilion, she said, the troops
had found the corpses of 300 to 400 commune members
stacked around the throne of Jim Jones. Hundreds of
people were unaccounted for, including Jones, she said.

Later that day, Charles A. Krause and Frank Johnston
of *The Washington Post* flew into the jungle for their own
inspection of the scene. Guyanese military officials put
the death toll at 398. Guyanese civilian officials used the
number 405. Krause's own estimate was about 400. He
found Jim Jones near his throne, dead from a gunshot
wound in the head. But others members of the cult whom
he had met on November 17 and 18 were nowhere to be
seen among the dead.

He reported in *The Post* the following day that
hundreds of the Jonestown settlers were unaccounted for
and there was "speculation that hundreds of people fled to
the jungle and simply have not found their way out. But
there was also another theory: that some of the Jonestown
security men took hundreds of the commune's residents
to a remote area, possibly to be shot. Lending some
support to that theory was the fact that Tom Kice, Sr.,
one of those believed to have been among the gunmen
who attacked Ryan's party, has not been found.

"Also, lawyers (Mark) Lane and (Charles) Garry, who
escaped into the forest when the killing began, reported
yesterday that they heard scattered screaming and
shooting in the forest while they were in hiding."

For days thereafter, the mystery of the missing cultists
deepened. A popular speculation was that they had
plunged into the jungle to hide out in the homes of

Amerindians, the aboriginal tribesmen who lived near
Jonestown and sometimes worked at the commune.
Another speculation was that the survivors were heading
for the Venezuelan border, only 20 miles from the Peoples
Temple. This was all given a color of authenticity by
Guyana's Police Commissioner, Lloyd Barker, who told
reporters on Tuesday, November 22:

"There are many (Indian) settlements in the Jonestown
area. There are also many footpaths leading to the
(Indian) villages. I expect many of those who ran away
rather than obey Jones can be found at these villages.
Others may have continued on to the Venezuelan border
which is about a two-day walk.

"Most of those who fled were working on the perimeter
of the 2,000-acre Jonestown settlement when he issued his
call (for suicide). They disappeared into the bush. I am
advised that, after the tension died down, some of these
people crept into Jonestown and took food and money
with them."

For every theory, there was a counter-theory. *The New
York Times* on November 22 cast doubt on the ability of
any Jonestown survivors to make it out of the jungle alive:

"The region is a bewildering tangle of rain forests laced
with streams, creeks, and marshes. It is home to the
poisonous bushmaster snake, the flesh-eating piranha
and the night-roaming jaguar, as well as clouds of
malaria-carrying mosquitoes, ticks, spiders, and electric
eels. The regional rainy season is expected to begin any
day now, and this would further complicate the search for
survivors."

Only two days later, *The Times* was more optimistic on
this score. It reported:

"The Jonestown area bears little resemblance to
Hollywood fantasies of a tropical jungle. (A local
horticulturist) offered these examples:

"The piranha, except for the smallest species that 'can
be troublesome,' do not harm people.

"There are some isolated cases of malaria, but there
has been no yellow fever for years.

"A bushmaster snake can kill a person if it is big

enough, but in most cases death is caused by an improperly applied tourniquet.

"There are few animals of any size, and the jaguar, fearsome in jungle lore, runs away from people."

There was more to all this than the mathematics of the body count at Jonestown. The whole cosmology of the Jim Jones movement was at stake. If every man, woman, and child at the Temple had followed him gladly to death on the White Night of November 18, then the image of Jones as a hated despot and the image of Jonestown as a concentration camp was shattered. The willing suicide of his entire flock would have been a form of vindication for him, the ultimate proof of the love and devotion he had claimed and so devoutly desired.

If, on the other hand, cadres of gunmen from the Temple had marched the missing hundreds into the jungle for mass executions, the charge of his critics that he was more the embodiment of Heinrich Himmler than of Jesus Christ would have found grisly support.

Finally, if hundreds from the Jonestown commune were alive out there in the jungle, other speculations could be drawn. For the fearful and the paranoid defectors from his Temple and for their allies, there was the possibility that these survivors would one day return to wreak vengeance on them in the name of Jim Jones and to re-establish the structure he had built.

The other possibility was that they would return to bear witness against him, to strip away the myths of his goodness and love.

There was yet another dimension to the mystery. It kept alive in the minds and emotions of all the friends and relatives of the missing the hope that those they loved would be found and returned to them to build new lives.

The theory of hope was the strongest and from Monday until Thursday, November 23, Guyanese search parties patrolled in the jungle around Jonestown seeking survivors. Helicopters equipped with loudspeakers flew over the rain forests, broadcasting appeals to survivors to come out to safety.

On Friday, the veil of mystery was lifted. U.S. Army

troops who had been recovering bodies all week from Jonestown discovered that the Guyanese had made a rather large mathematical mistake when they issued their body count estimate the previous Monday. Instead of the 400 bodies the Guyanese had counted, the Americans by late Friday had counted 775 and, before the week was out, they had found more than 900. There was, thus, no need for any further search in the jungle. There was no need to fear the re-emergence of vengeful squads of survivors who would get even with the enemies of Father Jones. There was no longer any possibility that "hundreds" of rebellious Temple members would reappear to point damning fingers at the leader of the flock. And there was no longer any basis for hope—by those who still clung to it—that their son or daughter or husband or wife or brother or sister would come back home.

Some did come out, of course—those who left Jonestown with Leo Ryan on the afternoon of November 18 and then survived the subsequent attack by Temple gunmen; those Temple members who, for one reason or another, were in Georgetown at the time of the ritualistic holocaust; and those stragglers who had, in fact, fled the Temple on the White Night and had survived to tell their stories. Altogether they numbered about 100.

The final body count, in mathematical terms, enlarged the dimensions of the Jonestown tragedy. But long before the last infant or adult had been placed in a body bag, tagged, counted, and airlifted to the United States, recriminations had begun and the search for scapegoats was underway.

The Guyanese government was indicted by some critics for a whole range of alleged sins and mistakes, from the ineptness of the troops sent to Jonestown to the original decision of the government to grant Jim Jones an asylum in the jungle. The American government was another target of anger and suspicion. Why had the State Department failed to investigate properly the allegations against Jim Jones and the true conditions at Jonestown? Why had the FBI, the Social Security Administration, the Federal Communications Commission, and other bureaucratic instruments failed to do their various duties with respect to the members of the Jones flock?

For the dead, it signified nothing. The problem at Jonestown was not who was to blame or why it happened. It was a problem of logistics. What was to be done with these bodies rotting in the tropical heat of the jungle?

The United States Department of State, predictably, established a "Guyana Task Force," headed by a career diplomat, John Bushnell, one of three Deputy Assistant Secretaries of State for Inter-American Affairs. Ordinarily, this assignment would have gone to another Deputy Assistant Secretary, Brandon Grove. But Grove was preoccupied with the threat of a civil war in Nicaragua. So the job went to Bushnell. His task force was organized into eight-hour shifts. Officials were brought in from the Department of Defense and the FBI.

The first major decision out of the Task Force was that the dead at Jonestown should be buried there by the Guyanese government.

The reasoning was three-fold. First, the bodies were decomposing rapidly. Second, the decomposed bodies posed a threat of a cholera outbreak. Third, U.S. aircraft and personnel on hand in Guyana should be used to search for survivors in the jungle, rather than for recovery and burial purposes.

The Task Force proposal was turned down by the Guyanese. They wanted nothing to do with recovery and burial. The dead were Americans and should be dealt with by the Americans—in America. The Yankees, in short, should clean up their own mess.

This was something the President of the United States and his White House staff could not personally accomplish. Nor could Secretary of State Cyrus Vance, nor his personal staff nor the staff of the Guyana Task Force.

It was the kind of job for which society has created a division of labor, a category of people who handle the dead. Morticians and firemen and policemen and rescue squads perform the domestic function. Abroad, it is done by the military, specifically the Graves Registration Unit of the Army and the Air Force crews who provide the transport. They collect and identify and embalm and package those who perish in distant wars and disasters arranged by Presidents and Secretaries of State and by other fateful forces, human and natural.

So on Sunday, November 19, the word went out from the Joint Chiefs of Staff at the Pentagon to assemble the men and women necessary to deal with the human wreckage Jim Jones had left behind. The Military Airlift Command in St. Louis was to provde the airplanes to bring the Americans home. The Readiness Command at McDill Air Force Base in Florida was to round up the medics to treat the wounded and specialists to handle the dead. Fort Bragg, North Carolina, provided the graves registration people. Fort Benning, Georgia, provided the medical teams. Altogether, 282 Army and Air Force personnel, most of them volunteers, were dispatched to Guyana to clean up the grisly mess at Jonestown. C-141 and C-130 transports were loaded with folded-up helicopters and trucks, communications gear, and other materials to work in the bush. Jolly Green Giants, the big helicopters that had hauled thousands of bodies from the battles of Vietnam, were brought in to shuttle the dead from Jonestown to Georgetown.

The fallen members of the flock would come home at last to the military mortuary at Dover, Delaware. There, 35 pathologists and 29 body identification specialists were waiting, brought in from around the country.

When Jim Jones or his lieutenants ordered the attack on Leo Ryan and his party and when Jim Jones called for the collective suicide of his flock, it is doubtful that the ultimate consequences were given careful consideration.

The precise outcome was known only to those left with the task of dealing with those consequences—the body handlers.

The dead from Jonestown came in a steady flow to Dover, Delaware, on C-141 transports, used ordinarily to transport troops and cargo. The mortuary at Dover had been built in the 1960s to handle similar assignments growing out of the war in Vietnam. The military contingent there, trained in the ceremonies of death, tried

at first to treat the incoming victims from Jonestown with
the rituals of respect. The first coffins were carried off by
squads moving with the slow, formal cadence prescribed
in the manuals. But there were too many bodies and by
Thursday, November 23, they were being handled like
cargoes of freight. A chaplain still prayed at the landing of
each plane. But the troops began stacking the containers
two and three deep on yellow, flat-bed trailers. The flight
crews began unloading them in groups of nine strapped
together, three deep and three high.

The stories were that, inside the coffins, the decomposition of bodies was awful. Limbs had fallen off. There
were infestations of maggots. The smell of rotten flesh
permeated the air.

There was more to be done. It was necessary to identify
the human remains inside these containers, a tedious
process under the best of conditions. Prints were needed
from all 10 fingers because of the absence of names or
identifying documents. The prints then had to be matched
with fingerprints in FBI files.

Around the clock, the mortuary crews went about the
grisly business. In many cases, the decomposition of flesh
was so advanced that the hands lacked the firmness to
make fingerprints. This forced the crews to remove the
upper layer of skin from each finger, slip it on their own
hands over rubber gloves, and make the inked impressions.

There was another problem. Body gases, expanding
from exposure to the sun and heat of the jungle, bloated
some of the forms and had to be released by incision
before the embalming process could begin. In many cases,
decomposition had broken down the veins that usually
carry embalming fluid. It was necessary to inject the fluid
into open body cavities.

All that was one of the legacies of Jonestown. Jim
Jones had often told his followers that there was beauty in
death. In the final moments, exhorting them to take their
own lives, he cried out:

"It is time to die with dignity."

There was no beauty, no dignity in the aftermath of

that White Night. There was only death and its rot. And even that was not the end of it. The sorrow and dark questionings had only begun. The search for scapegoats was underway.

15.

"The jungle is only a few yards away."

The jungle Arcadia of Reverend James Jones and his followers is now empty and still. Perhaps it would be most fitting if its domain were now taken back by the jungle, the jaguar, and the bushmaster snake. Instead of becoming the model human habitation he professed it to be, Jonestown caused the world to draw its breath in horror.

There is sure to be a search for scapegoats. Congressional investigations have already been threatened. Relatives of the dead who had flown desperately to Georgetown, Guyana, ask with helpless grief what point there is in being an American if we had no power to avert such a thing. The implication was that there was *something* the government should have done. These were after all more than 900 American citizens...

Why did the Federal Communications Commission permit the Temple to operate its ham radio frequency between San Francisco and Guyana as a channel for carrying out Jones's nefarious designs? Why didn't the State Department find out that members of the colony were being kept against their will, were being beaten and punished in underground boxes? Why were social security checks being mailed to the colony when proceeds were being appropriated by Jones and his inner circle? Why wasn't the FBI or the CIA on the case?

These were understandable questions and sentiments. But the State Department official who responded, "We're not babysitters"—probably had it right. It is not the duty of the American government to interfere with the lives of its citizens abroad so long as they conduct themselves in a peaceful and lawful manner. Less yet is it the government's duty to protect American citizens from each other.

This, too, was not unreasonable. After all it has been only a few years since the intrusions of U.S. intelligence agencies into the lives of private citizens was being decried in Congress, apologized for by high-ranking CIA and FBI officials and decried on editorial pages across the nation.

Yet the inevitable quest for a scapegoat will be pressed by some in the hope that it will atone for the offense or that it will, somehow, prevent it from happening again. The State Department has been accused of failing to snoop more effectively into the affairs of the Jones cult. (Another group called the House of Israel, composed of black American Jews, has settled in Guyana, but escaped attention in the furor.) The political opposition to Guyanan Prime Minister Forbes Burnham has accused him of maintaining secret links to Jones.

But the fact remains that several hundred adult Americans of their own free will followed Jones to Guyana. Many of them voluntarily swallowed the fatal potion of cyanide and died. Not the same can be said for their young children who were denied the opportunity for a full life. Here, too, the only blame that can be assessed would have to be against the dead parents. If Jones was ultimately responsible for forcing them all to their deaths—whether with guns or brain-washing—then he, too, is beyond the punishment now of any civil authority.

It is only human to try to make some sense of all this. Is there not a moral to be drawn, even from an event so profoundly aberrational? From each corner of the world already have come efforts to explain and moralize for the holocaust—from each country according to its separate visions.

Tass, the official Soviet news agency, was quick to attribute the "bloody events" in Guyana to the fact that "millions are the victims of an inhumane society" in the United States.

The Swiss responded to the tragedy with austerity: "Only the active support of famous Americans enabled the murder sect to build up their piece of devilry," said Zurich's *Der Blick* under a headline saying "Jimmy Carter's Wife Supported Mad Sect." Echoed *Tages-Anzeiger* of Zurich: "The fact that Jim Jones was sent to the fringe of the jungle with letters of recommendation from prominent U.S. personalities speaks for itself."

The Manila *Daily Express* took the opportunity to sink a barb into the American press. "If you have been reading the gory details of this story," wrote the newspaper's columnist Teodoro Valencia, "you'll have noticed how carefully the American press has treated it as plain reportage. If the cultists had been Filipinos, the Western press would have pictured them as uncivilized and sadistic. This is a perfect example of 'truth' in American journalism..."

The international stereotype of California as the home of American mysticism and cult was reflected in the flow of editorial opinion.

"The grotesque mass suicides cannot be looked upon as an isolated nightmare," wrote Stockholm's *Dagens Nyheter*. "There is a connection with the social and political development of a large generation of people, above all in California...The individual way of self-fulfillment has included more of drugs, of extreme religiousness, and of sexual experiments. The demand for new sensations has gradually increased...In the hunt for new happenings, death becomes the last absolute trip..."

Tokyo's *Asahi Shimbun* simply asks: "Is there anything hidden in California that brings about lunacy?"

Suddeutsche Zeitung of Munich reacted with a characteristically German note of scholarly analysis: "American society is composed of joiners, of people who

like to form associations. The German sociologist Max
Weber, when he was in America in 1905, tried to explain
this voluntary joining as a passage from the closed,
structured old world to the tense individualism of the
new. Demons like he (Jones) appear again and again to
thrive in the California climate; before him was, for
example, the black field marshal General Cinque, whose
group kidnapped Patty Hearst."

The *Straits Times* of Singapore said "America still
suffers from the backwash of the utopia-seeking sixties,"
while *Kyunghyang* of Seoul, Korea, blames it on the fact
that "men's minds have been driven by the material
civilization into hollowness."

In the American press there was the inevitable rush to
the "quote" circuits of psychiatric opinion for instant
diagnosis of Jones, of his followers, and of cult behavior
generally. Yale's Dr. Robert J. Lifton, front-runner by
many lengths in the quotational sweep-stakes, epitomized
the conventional wisdom with such observations as this:
"When people are facing dislocations of rapid social
change and the present looks frightening, there is often a
cry for a return to absolute simplicity in the rules of
living." Suicide, he said, may be a way of immortalizing
these fundamentalist principles when they are under
attack from outside.

Confronted with this flood of instant sociological
analysis, *Washington Post* columnist William Raspberry
found himself wondering whether "maybe we would be
better off simply accepting the fact that some tragedies
cannot be prevented. I don't mean that there should be no
effort to understand the dynamics of cultism, of
alienation, or of group suicide...But I do make a
distinction between scientific inquiry aimed at discover-
ing truth and ritual questioning calculated to restore our
sense of equilibrium."

One of the diverting sideshows to the central tragedy of
the events in Jonestown was the appearance on the scene
of attorney Mark Lane, who has managed to vamp his
way into the most traumatic episodes of recent American
history. Lane, entrepreneur of conspiracy theories in the

John F. Kennedy and Martin Luther King, Jr., assassinations, was hired by Jones to fend off government conspiracies against the Peoples Temple and its jungle commune in Guyana. Jones retained the flamboyant New Yorker when he became dissatisfied with the services of Charles Garry of San Francisco, long-standing counsel to the Black Panthers.

Hardly had he emerged from the jungle where he and Garry took refuge once the ritual suicides and killings began at Jonestown, when Lane began expounding new theories of conspiracy incriminating his late client, Reverend Jones. Lane charged that the mass suicide in Guyana was the first step in a master plan financed by a secret $10 million trust fund to carry out assassinations of other U.S. public officials.

It was in an airborne interview with *The Washington Post* after the killing that Lane casually acknowledged that he knew people were being kept in Jonestown against their will, when necessary with strong depressants and tranquilizers. Earlier Lane had portrayed Jones and his followers as victims of unfair publicity and the targets of a conspiracy by U.S. government agencies.

The lawyer also confessed that even before Ryan's visit he knew that Jones was sick, that the atmosphere in Jonestown was explosive and that the paranoid leader was serious about taking his followers to their deaths. An infuriated relative, upon learning of Lane's claim to prior knowledge, bitterly accused the attorney of "complicity in the crime."

As of last reports, Lane was planning to write a book. In the jungle, as the suicides were beginning, Lane later related, he persuaded his and Garry's armed guard to let them escape so that "I will be able to tell the world about the last moments of Jonestown."

In the end, we will have to accept what happened in Guyana as the dark spasm of history that it was, a tragedy in which fates were assigned both by chance and by inevitable circumstance, beyond the control of any government agency or political party.

Undoubtedly, it will be probed by historians, psychologists, and politicians for whatever prescriptive wisdom it may afford. Today, it simply haunts us, as *Newsweek* columnist Meg Greenfield observed, with its reminder that "the jungle is only a few yards away."

CHRONOLOGY

Chronology

May 13, 1931: James Warren Jones is born near Lynn, Indiana. He is the only child of James T. Jones, an invalid who was gassed in combat during World War I, and Lynetta Jones, sometime waitress and factory worker.

1949: Jones graduates from Richmond (Indiana) High School and marries Marceline Baldwin, nurse.

1950: Jones enrolls in Indiana University. Described at the time as "maladjusted," he leaves school and becomes involved with an Indianapolis fundamentalist congregation and serves as its occasional preacher.

1951: Jones enrolls in Butler University, then run by the Christian Church (Disciples of Christ). He does not receive his B.S. in education until 1961.

1953: Jones founds his own interdenominational Christian Assembly of God church.

1960: The Christian Church (Disciples of Christ) of Indianapolis lists Jones's The Peoples Temple Full Gospel Church as one of its congregations.

1961: Leo J. Ryan is elected mayor of South San Francisco. Jones is named director of the Indianapolis Human Rights Commission.

1962: Leo J. Ryan is elected to the California State Legislature.

1964: Jim Jones is ordained as a minister in the Christian Church (Disciples of Christ).

1965: Jones sets up two corporations, his first serious money-making ventures. The nonprofit Wings of Deliverance, registers its purpose with the IRS as "furthering the Kingdom of God and spreading the true Holy Word of God." Jim-Lu-Mar Corp.'s stated purpose is making money by the acquisition of enterprises. The Indiana secretary of state revokes the corporate licenses of both in 1970 for failing to file annual reports.

1965: Jones claims having a vision of nuclear holocaust which is slated to happen on July 15, 1967. Citing an *Esquire* magazine article, Jones claims northern California would be safe from both a bomb blast and lingering nuclear fallout. He and 150 followers move to Ukiah, California, but Jones continues to visit the Temple in Indiana, where he claims to resurrect the dead and purge the faithful of cancers.

Jones is named foreman of the Mendocino County (California) grand jury.

Leo J. Ryan goes undercover to Watts as a high school teacher in the aftermath of the riots. This year, he also travels to Newfoundland to investigate the hunting of harp seal pups.

1971: The Peoples Temple buys churches in Los Angeles and San Francisco where Jones wins a following mainly among inner-city blacks and liberal whites who are attracted to the Temple's dazzling activities, a mixture of soul and gospel services, day and health care, radical politics and good works.

1971: The Indiana State Psychology Board looks into claims allegedly made by Jones that he could cure "psychosomatic diseases," but no resultant action is taken by the board.

1973: January—Leo J. Ryan enters Congress as the Democratic Representative from California's San Mateo County.

January—The Peoples Temple donates $4,400 to twelve newspapers in a well-publicized gesture in "defense of a free press."

December—Jones is arrested in a Hollywood theater on a lewd conduct charge after an undercover policeman says Jones tried to molest him. The charge is dismissed in a dispute over the legality of the arrest. It is not reported in the press.

December—Jonestown, the Peoples Temple colony in Guyana, is founded.

1975: May—The Peoples Temple gives $300 toward the defense of the "*Fresno Bee* Four," newsmen facing jail for refusing to reveal their news sources.

May—Jones is named one of the 100 most outstanding clergymen in the nation by Religion in American Life, an inter-faith organization.

1976: January—The Peoples Temple gives $6,000 to the San Francisco Senior Assistance program, a service organization aiding elderly residents of San Francisco's Tenderloin district.

January—Jones is named "Humanitarian of the Year" by the *Los Angeles Herald.*

September—Ten busloads of Peoples Temple members picket the Fresno County Courthouse to protest the jailing of the "*Fresno Bee* Four."

October—Jones is appointed to the San Francisco Housing Authority by San Francisco Mayor George Moscone.

October—Cult member Bob Houston announces his intention to leave the Peoples Temple. That night he is found dead and mangled next to the San Francisco railroad tracks.

1977: January—Jones receives the annual Martin Luther King, Jr., Humanitarian Award in San Francisco.

February—Jones becomes chairman of the San Francisco Housing Authority.

July—San Francisco lawyer Charles E. Garry takes on a new client—the Peoples Temple.

July—Rumors of *New West* Magazine's intention to publish an investigative story on the Peoples Temple spark a flurry of attempts to stop the story by Temple members and local San Francisco politicians.

July—*New West*, in its August 1 issue, publishes damning accounts of life in the Peoples Temple. City Supervisor Quentin Kopp asks for an official investigation, but is denied by Mayor Moscone.

August—Jones resigns as head of the San Francisco Housing Authority. The resignation is dictated by short-wave radio from Guyana.

August—San Francisco District Attorney Joseph Freitas orders a review of all Peoples Temple activities. The review is inconclusive.

August—Al and Jeannie Mills sue the Peoples Temple for $1.1 million charging that they were beaten and cheated of their property by the sect.

1978: April—Relatives of Jonestown cultists issue a statement accusing Jones of human rights violations and quoting him as saying, "... We are devoted to a decision that it is better even to die than to be constantly harrassed from one continent to the next."

June—Deborah Layton Blakey, former cult member, writes an affidavit testifying to conditions at Jonestown. She warns of colonists' suicide rehearsals and pacts.

June—James Cobb files suit against Jones in San Francisco charging Jones with planning "mass murder" that "would result in the death of minor children not old enough to make voluntary and informed decisions about serious matters of any nature, much less insane proposals of collective suicide."

November 7—U.S. consular officials in Guyana make the latest of four visits to Jonestown in 1978. After interviewing Temple members, they report "not one confirmation of any allegation of mistreatment," according to a State Department spokesman.

Monday, November 13—Charles Krause receives the assignment to cover Leo Ryan's trip to the Jonestown colony. Ryan is traveling as a member of the House International Affairs Committee and on behalf of his constituents to look into conditions at Jonestown. He is to be accompanied by members of the Concerned Relatives group as well as the press.

In Georgetown, Guyana, the Peoples Temple issues a release to the local press saying the Jonestown community had voted not to permit a visit by Concerned Relatives, charging them with having "stepped up (their) malicious, year-round campaign of lies and harrassment."

Tuesday, November 14—Ryan leaves New York, bound for Guyana. He is accompanied by 13 members of Concerned Relatives, the NBC film crew, the San Francisco journalists, and two aides. Krause joins up with Ryan's party in Trinidad and they continue on to Georgetown's Timehri airport.

Wednesday, November 15—Ryan and party arrive in Georgetown shortly after midnight, Wednesday morning. The journalists spend the day in bureaucratic hassles at the airport and hotels.

Ryan visits the Georgetown headquarters of the Peoples Temple. Negotiations continue to allow the delegation to visit Jonestown.

Ryan receives a petition from Jonestown telling the delegation to stay away. It is signed with 600 names.

Thursday, November 16—The Peoples Temple issues a local press release saying it "reserves the right not to entertain the U.S. delegation. However, we feel that Mr. Ryan will easily see through the gross misportrayals, lies and false charges...if he is an honest and objective person."

The Ryan delegation learns that lawyers Mark Lane and Charles Garry are on their way to Guyana at Jones's request.

Friday, November 17—Ryan announces that he intends to go to Jonestown, taking along his entourage, whether or not Jonestown gives permission.

By early afternoon, Jones's lawyers have arrived in Georgetown and permission is granted.

The visitors to Jonestown are:

Representative Leo J. Ryan and aide Jacqueline Speier;

U.S. Embassy deputy chief of mission Richard Dwyer;

Jones's lawyers Charles E. Garry and Mark Lane;

Guyanese government information officer Neville Annibourne;

Concerned Relatives Carol Boyd, Jim Cobb, Anthony Katsaris, and Beverly Oliver;

and Charles Krause, *The Washington Post*; Tim Reiterman and Greg Robinson, *San Francisco Examiner*; Ron Javers, *San Francisco Chronicle*; Steve Sung, Don Harris, Bob Brown, and Bob Flick, NBC; and Gordon Lindsay, freelance.

After an afternoon and evening of entertainment and interviews, Ryan and aides spend the night in Jonestown. The journalists and Concerned Relatives return to Port Kaituma for the night.

Harris and Ryan are given notes from community members who want to leave.

Saturday, November 18—In the morning, Ryan resumes interviewing Jonestown's residents while the journalists tour the settlement.

By early afternoon the group is preparing to leave. Suddenly Ryan is attacked by a knife-wielding cultist, Don Sly. Ryan escapes unharmed.

A few minutes after 4:00 P.M., just as they prepare to board two airplanes at Port Kaituma airport, Ryan's party is attacked by members of the settlement. The assailants, firing pistols and automatic weapons, kill Ryan, Harris, Brown, Robinson, and escaping cultist, Patricia Parks.

Wounded are Dwyer, Speier, Sung, Javers, Reiterman, Krause, and the following colony members or relatives of members: Vernon Gosney, Monica Bagby, Anthony Katsaris, Beverly Oliver, and Carol Boyd.

Shortly after 5:00 P.M. Jones gives the order for the "White Night." This is no rehearsal. When the bodies are finally counted the death toll is over 900.

APPENDICES

APPENDIX A
The Justice Department Replies...

Thank you for your letter of January 10, 1977, enclosing copies of correspondence received by the Committee on the Judiciary concerning the Unification Church and other religious sects.

The Department of Justice has received numerous complaints from distressed parents of members of various religious sects, alleging that their adult children are the victims of "brainwashing," "mind control," or "mental kidnaping" by leaders of these groups. Typically, the parents allege that new members of these sects are subjected to intensive indoctrination, accompanied by inadequate amounts of sleep and food, with the result that the new members become "programmed" to obey the wishes and commands of the sect leaders, and cease thinking for themselves.

As you know, the First Amendment's protection of religious freedom embraces the right to maintain religious beliefs which are rank heresy to followers of orthodox faiths. *United States* v. *Ballard,* 322 U.S. 78. The Department of Justice cannot conduct a general inquiry into the activities of a religious group. Any investigation must be predicated on an allegation of a violation of Federal law.

A great deal of consideration has been given to this situation, particularly to the possibility that the imposition of mental restraints upon the freedom of movement of a sect member might constitute a violation of the Federal kidnaping statute, 18 U.S.C. 1201. In *Chatwin* v. *United States*, 326 U.S. 455, the Supreme Court, in considering the Federal kidnaping statute, recognized that an unlawful restraint could be achieved by mental as well as by physical means. However, the restraint must be against the victim's will, and with a willful intent to confine the victim. It seems clear that the Court will not construe the kidnaping statute so as to punish one individual who induces another to leave his surroundings to do some innocent or illegal act, state lines subsequently being crossed. 326 U.S. at 464. In *Chatwin*, the defendants, members of a Mormon cult, persuaded a 15-year-old mentally retarded girl that a "celestial" or plural marriage was essential to her salvation, and she was taken interstate to consummate such a marriage. Subsequently, the defendants were convicted under the kidnaping statute. The Supreme Court, in reversing the convictions, concluded that there was no evidence that the victim had been confined against her will or that she lacked the mental capacity to understand the concept of "celestial" marriage and to exercise her own free will in this regard. In short, the purpose of the statute is to outlaw interstate kidnaping rather than general transgressions of morality involving the crossing of state lines. Therefore, it seems clear that a prosecution under the kidnaping statute could not be sustained based on evidence that an adult of normal intelligence had been "brainwashed" into continued association with a religious sect.

We have also considered the possibility that these allegations amount to violations of other Federal criminal statutes pertaining to peonage, slavery, and involuntary servitude. 13 U.S.C. 1581 prohibits holding or returning any person to a condition of peonage. The gravemen of this offense is the holding of another to labor in satisfaction of a debt. *United States* v. *Gaskin*, 320 U.S. 527. This obviously does not apply to a situation in which a member is induced to work for a sect. With regard to 18 U.S.C. 1583 and 1584, which prohibit slavery and involuntary servitude, the victim must have or believe that he has no way to avoid continued service or confinement. If the victim has a choice between freedom and confinement, even if the choice of freedom entails what he believes to be serious consequences, there is no violation. See *United States* v. *Shackney*, 333 F. 2d 475 (2nd Cir., 1964).

In order to initiate a Federal criminal investigation under the kidnaping statute or under 18 U.S.C. 1583 and 1584, of individuals alleged to have subjected religious sect members to "brainwashing," there must be information or an allegation that the victim was actually deprived of his liberty against his will by physical or mental restraints. Allegations that the victim was induced, persuaded, proselytized, or "brainwashed" to voluntarily continue his association with the sect would be insufficient. In the case of a kidnaping investigation, there would also have to be information or an allegation that the victim was being held for ransom, reward, or otherwise and that the jurisdictional element of interstate travel was present.

Consideration has also been given to the possibility of new legislation in this area. However, any legislation which would intervene in the practices of a sect would be an infringement of the sect's free exercise of religion. The free exercise of religion guaranteed by the First Amendment embraces two concepts: the freedom to believe and the freedom to act. The freedom to believe is absolute, but religious activity may be subject to regulation for the protection of society. *Cantwell* v. *Connecticut*, 310 U.S. 296. Legal restrictions, however, cannot be placed on religious activities in the same manner that they may be applied to secular activities. The power of the Government to regulate secular activities, so far as due process is concerned, includes the power to impose all of the restrictions which a legislature has a

rational basis for adopting. However, religious activity
may not be restricted on such narrow grounds. It is
susceptible of restriction only to prevent grave and
immediate dangers to interests which Government may
lawfully protect. *Sherbert* v. *Verner*, 374 U.S. 398,
Church of Scientology v. *United States* 409 F. 2d 1146
(D.C. Cir., 1969) cert. denied 396 U.S. 963.

Even if a sect requires its members to undergo long
hours of training and indoctrination with limited
amounts of food and sleep, it is questionable that this
activity presents a grave and immediate danger either to
society or the member, so as to warrant the imposition of
Federal criminal sanctions. This problem is further
complicated by the difficulty, if not impossibility, of
determining whether a member conforms his actions to
the dictates of a sect leader because of a sincere religious
belief that the leader speaks the will of God, or because
the member is merely a victim of "brainwashing." Any
legislation which sought to restrict religious activity on
the basis that sect members' adherence to the religion was
based on "brainwashing" would seem to require a finding
that the members' religious beliefs were false. Judicial
determination of the truth or falsity of religious beliefs
has been rejected by the Supreme Court. See *Ballard,
supra.* Therefore, it appears that the possibility of
drafting effective Federal criminal legislation in this area
is most unlikely.

I understand that some parents of sect members have
had success in pursuing civil remedies involving court
appointments as guardians or conservators for their adult
children. Recently, the parents of a 22-year-old Unification Church member secured custody of their son after
obtaining a court order from the District of Columbia
Superior Court permitting the parents to take their son
into custody to be counseled, examined and treated by
psychiatrists, social workers and doctors, and to keep him
in custody until there was a hearing on the matter.
Additionally, in a case entitled *Helander* v. *Unification
Church*, et al., in the District of Columbia Superior Court
Family Division the parents of a sect member petitioned

for a writ of Habeas Corpus. Although the court held that there was insufficient evidence to establish that the sect member had been restrained from her lawful liberty by the sect, it appears that with a sufficient showing, Habeas Corpus is another remedy in these situations. In view of the more stringent burden of proof required in criminal prosecutions, it seems clear that aggrieved parents would have a greater likelihood of success in pursuing civil remedies rather than requesting criminal prosecutions in these situations.

Finally, I would like to point out that the Department has received a number of complaints from adult members of religious sects alleging that they have been abducted by their parents or persons acting on behalf of their parents, and subjected to "deprogramming," a process which purports to free the sect member from his "brainwashed" condition. Where these complaints raise an allegation of a violation of Federal law, appropriate investigations are conducted.

APPENDIX B

GRC:ALH:AFN:mac
146-1-0
Retyped: 7/19/77

July 29, 1977

Honorable Robert N. Giaimo
House of Representatives
Washington, D.C.

Dear Congressman Giaimo:

Thank you for your letter of June 24, 1977.

Since your meeting on May 18, 1977, with representatives of the Criminal Division, we have reviewed the manuscript submitted by Professor Richard Delgado. In addition, the FBI, at our request, contacted Dr. Margaret Singer, who was unable to provide any specific data. As a result we have requested the FBI to interview 18 other persons who may possibly possess information relating to criminal activity by persons associated with religious sects. In connection with these interviews, the FBI is being requested to determine: (1) if the individual was actually physically restrained by any religious sect, or (2) if the individual was actually present and observed another being physically restrained by any religious sect. The FBI has been instructed to limit the interviews to this area of inquiry and that it should be made clear to the

Records
Gen. Crimes Sec.
Mr. Norton (2)
Mr. Civiletti
Chrono

interviewees that the FBI is not conducting a general inquiry into the activities or religious practices of any religious sect.

It continues to be the position of the Criminal Division that allegations of "brainwashing," "mind control," "thought reform" or "coercive persuasion" would not support a prosecution under the Federal kidnaping statute. We are brought to this conclusion by the statute and its judicial interpretation. In *Chatwin* v. *United States*, 326 U.S. 455, the defendants, members of a Mormon cult persuaded a 15 year old mentally retarded girl that a "celestial" or plural marriage was essential to her salvation and she was taken interstate to consummate such a marriage. Subsequently, the defendants were convicted under the Federal kidnaping statute. The Supreme Court, in reversing the convictions, concluded that there was no evidence that the victim had been confined against her will or that she lacked the mental capacity to understand the concept of "celestial" marriage and to exercise her own free will in this regard. In short, the purpose of the statute is to outlaw interstate kidnapings rather than general transgressions of morality involving the crossing of state lines. Therefore, in our view, a prosecution under the kidnaping statute could not be sustained based on evidence that an adult of normal intelligence had been "brainwashed" into continued association with a religious sect. Similarly, it continues to be our position that these allegations would not be sufficient to sustain Federal criminal prosecutions under statutes pertaining to peonage, slavery, and involuntary servitude.

We are aware of only one criminal prosecution based on an allegation of "brainwashing." In *People of the State of New York* v. *ISKCON, Inc., et al.,* Queens County Supreme Court Nos. 2114-76, 2012-76, the defendants were charged with false imprisonment in the first degree. The prosecution's theory was that defendants, leaders of the Hare Krishna organization, falsely imprisoned members by deception and intimidation. In dismissing the indictment, the court said:

Religious proselytizing and the recruitment of and maintenance of belief through a strict regimen, meditation, chanting, self-denial and the communication of other religious teachings cannot under our laws—as presently enacted—be construed as criminal in nature and serve as the basis for a criminal indictment.

* * *

To sustain this indictment would open the so-called "Pandora's Box" to a plethora of unjustified investigations, accusations, and prosecutions that would go on ad infinitum, to the detriment of the citizens of our State and place in jeopardy our Federal and State Constitutions.

We have considered the possibility of new legislation in this area. However, any legislation which would intervene in the practices of a religious sect would be an infringement of the sect's free exercise of religion. The free exercise of religion guaranteed by the First Amendment embraces two concepts: the freedom to believe and the freedom to act. The freedom to believe is absolute, but the freedom to act may be subject to regulation for the protection of society. *Cantwell* v. *Connecticut*, 310 U.S. 296. Legal restrictions, however, cannot be placed on religious activity in the same manner that they may be applied to secular activities. The power of the government to regulate secular activities, so far as due process is concerned, includes the power to impose all of the restrictions which a legislature has a rational basis for adopting. However, religious activity may not be restricted on such grounds. It is susceptible of restriction only to prevent grave and immediate dangers to interests which government may lawfully protect. *Sherbert* v. *Verner*, 374 U.S. 398; *Church of Scientology* v. *United States*, 409 F. 2d 1146 (D.C. Cir., 1969) cert. denied 396 U.S. 963.

Even if a sect requires its members to undergo long
hours of work, training, and indoctrination with limited
amounts of food and sleep, it is questionable that these
activities present a grave and immediate danger either to
society or the member so as to warrant the imposition of
Federal criminal sanctions. This problem is further
complicated by the difficulty, if not impossibility, of
determining whether a member conforms his actions to
the dictates of a sect leader because of a sincere religious
belief that the leader speaks the will of God, or because
the member is merely a victim of "brainwashing." Any
legislation which sought to restrict religious activity on
the basis that sect members' adherence to the religion was
based on "brainwashing" would seem to require a finding
that the members' religious beliefs were false. Judicial
determination of the truth or falsity of religious beliefs
has been rejected by the Supreme Court. *United States* v.
Ballard, 322 U.S. 78.

As Professor Delgado correctly points out in his
manuscript, any government intervention in the practices
of a religious sect must be based on a showing of "societal
harm," and the degree of "societal harm" must be
balanced against the interest of the sect in practicing its
religion. Under this balancing test, any government
intervention in religious activities should be of the least
onerous kind so as to correct the "societal harm" and at
the same time recognize the interests of the sect in
practicing its religion. The imposition of criminal
sanctions, of course, is the harshest form of intervention
that the government can impose.

It has been our experience that members of these
religious sects are apparently competent, consenting
adults. In our view, evidence that sect members do not
have the capacity to exercise a free will is inconclusive.
Even if it can be shown that sect members' consent has
been diminished by the sect, we believe that this is the kind
of wrong which should be corrected by remedies less
onerous than Federal criminal sanctions.

Professor Delgado suggests certain preventive remedies such as disclosure requirements for certain religious
sects. Such requirements, of course, invite Constitutional

challenges. He also suggests post induction remedies such as tort actions and conservatorship proceedings. As you know, a number of parents have used state conservatorship laws to obtain custody of their adult children for purposes of "deprogramming." The validity of these conservatorship proceedings is now being challenged in the courts.

We recognize the hurt that parents suffer when their adult children give up their former way of life to join a religious sect. It is our position, however, that this is not a subject for judicial scrutiny by way of the Federal criminal justice system.

I hope the foregoing information clarifies our position on this subject.

Very truly yours,

Benjamin R. Civiletti
Assistant Attorney General
Criminal Division

By:

Robert L. Keuch
Deputy Assistant Attorney General
Criminal Division

APPENDIX C

Department of Justice

FOR IMMEDIATE RELEASE   DAG
FRIDAY, NOVEMBER 24, 1978   202-633-2014

Deputy Attorney General Benjamin R. Civiletti today issued the following statement on behalf of the Department of Justice on Department policy in investigating allegations of criminal activity by persons associated with religious sects:

On May 18, 1977, Deputy Assistant Attorney General Robert L. Keuch and other representatives of the Criminal Division met with Congressmen Robert Giaimo and Leo Ryan; Professor Richard Delgado of the University of Washington Law School; Dr. Margaret Singer, a psychologist from Berkeley, California, and Dr. Colin Williams of the Yale Divinity School. The purpose of the meeting was to discuss "brainwashing" as allegedly practiced by some religious sects. The People's Temple was never mentioned.

The participants at the meeting were advised that the Criminal Division had been aware of allegations of "brainwashing" by religious sects and that it had given serious study and review to the complaints. It was emphasized, however, that the Department of Justice must operate within the constraints of the federal criminal law and the First Amendment and that the courts had traditionally afforded a high degree of protection to religious activities.

The position of the Criminal Division has been and continues to be that allegations of "brainwashing" alone would not support criminal investigations and prosecu-

tions under the Federal Kidnapping Statute or other
federal criminal statutes pertaining to peonage, slavery,
or involuntary servitude. This position is based in part on
the Supreme Court's decision in *Chatwin* v. *U.S.*, 326
U.S. 466. The Department is releasing two letters that
thoroughly explain its position in this matter.

Subsequent to the May 18 meeting, Dr. Singer
furnished the names of several individuals that she
believed had been restrained against their will by religious
sects or had first-hand information of such restraints. The
FBI was requested by the Criminal Division to conduct
interviews of these individuals. As a result, the FBI
interviewed some 18 individuals. However, no information was developed which furnished a basis for federal
criminal jurisdiction or warranted further investigation.

The Department of Justice has never rebuffed
complaints from members of Congress or from others
that federal laws might have been violated by persons
connected with religious sects. We have made numerous
inquiries into such allegations. In some cases, we have
concluded there were no federal violations. In a few, we
have turned over information developed to the appropriate state authorities. In all cases, we have made clear that
the Department was not and could not lawfully conduct a
general inquiry into the activities or practices of any
religious sects.

Contrary to a *New York Times* report, Deputy
Attorney General Civiletti never met with the group
referred to above on May 18, 1977. Nor did Deputy
Attorney General Civiletti write, sign, or personally see
the letter to which the article referred, although the letter
is consistent with the law and long-standing Department
policy. It was issued from the Assistant Attorney
General's office and within the authority of its author and
signer Deputy Assistant Attorney General Robert L.
Keuch.

The Department of Justice recognizes the anguish that
parents suffer when their adult children give up their
former way of life to join a different religious sect.
However, in enforcing the federal criminal law we must

act within our jurisdiction and scrupulously observe constitutional restraints.

The Department of Justice shares the grief and shock of the families, friends and of the nation arising out of the mass tragedy occurring within the past week in Guyana. It has begun already and will do everything within its powers to investigate these occurrences so that the perpetrators and participants, wherever located, can be brought to justice. We are making this effort in conjunction with the State Department, consistent with international law and the cooperation of the sovereign state of Guyana. In addition, we are assisting other departments and agencies of the United States government in a combined effort to properly identify and return the bodies of the victims and to secure the personal property involved. We are working urgently with the State Department and other agencies to provide for the safe and prompt return of survivors consistent with legitimate investigatory needs.

APPENDIX D

AFFIDAVIT OF DEBORAH LAYTON BLAKEY RE THE THREAT AND POSSIBILITY OF MASS SUICIDE BY MEMBERS OF THE PEOPLE'S TEMPLE

I, DEBORAH LAYTON BLAKEY, declare the following under penalty of perjury:

1. The purpose of this affidavit is to call to the attention of the United States government the existence of a situation which threatens the lives of United States citizens living in Jonestown, Guyana.

2. From August, 1971 until May 13, 1978, I was a member of the People's Temple. For a substantial period of time prior to my departure for Guyana in December, 1977, I held the position of Financial Secretary of the People's Temple.

3. I was 18 years old when I joined the People's Temple. I had grown up in affluent circumstances in the permissive atmosphere of Berkeley, California. By joining the People's Temple, I hoped to help others and in the process to bring structure and self-discipline to my own life.

4. During the years I was a member of the People's Temple, I watched the organization depart with increasing frequency from its professed dedication to social change and participatory democracy. The Rev. Jim Jones gradually assumed a tyrannical hold over the lives of Temple members.

5. Any disagreement with his dictates came to be regarded as "treason". The Rev. Jones labelled any person who left the organization a "traitor" and "fair game". He steadfastly and convincingly maintained that the punishment for defection was death. The fact that severe corporal punishment was frequently administered

to Temple members gave the threats a frightening air of reality.

6. The Rev. Jones saw himself as the center of a conspiracy. The identity of the conspirators changed from day to day along with his erratic world vision. He induced the fear in others that, through their contact with him, they had become targets of the conspiracy. He convinced black Temple members that if they did not follow him to Guyana, they would be put into concentration camps and killed. White members were instilled with the belief that their names appeared on a secret list of enemies of the state that was kept by the C.I.A. and that they would be tracked down, tortured, imprisoned, and subsequently killed if they did not flee to Guyana.

7. Frequently, at Temple meetings, Rev. Jones would talk non-stop for hours. At various times, he claimed that he was the reincarnation of either Lenin, Jesus Christ, or one of a variety of other religious or political figures. He claimed that he had divine powers and could heal the sick. He stated that he had extrasensory perception and could tell what everyone was thinking. He said that he had powerful connections the world over, including the Mafia, Idi Amin, and the Soviet government.

8. When I first joined the Temple, Rev. Jones seemed to make clear distinctions between fantasy and reality. I believed that most of the time when he said irrational things, he was aware that they were irrational, but that they served as a tool of his leadership. His theory was that the end justified the means. At other times, he appeared to be deluded by a paranoid vision of the world. He would not sleep for days at a time and talk compulsively about the conspiracies against him. However, as time went on, he appeared to become genuinely irrational.

9. Rev. Jones insisted that Temple members work long hours and completely give up all semblance of a personal life. Proof of loyalty to Jones was confirmed by actions showing that a member had given up everything, even basic necessities. The most loyal were in the worst physical condition. Dark circles under one's eyes or extreme loss of weight were considered signs of loyalty.

10. The primary emotions I came to experience were exhaustion and fear. I knew that Rev. Jones was in some sense "sick", but that did not make me any less afraid of him.

11. Rev. Jones fled the United States in June, 1977 amidst growing public criticism of the practices of the Temple. He informed members of the Temple that he would be imprisoned for life if he did not leave immediately.

12. Between June, 1977 and December, 1977, when I was ordered to depart from Guyana, I had access to coded radio broadcasts from Rev. Jones in Guyana to the People's Temple headquarters in San Francisco.

13. In September, 1977, an event which Rev. Jones viewed as a major crisis occurred. Through listening to coded radio broadcasts and conversations with other members of the Temple staff, I learned that an attorney for former Temple member Grace Stoen had arrived in Guyana, seeking the return of her son, John Victor Stoen.

14. Rev. Jones has expressed particular bitterness toward Grace Stoen. She had been Chief Counselor, a position of great responsibility within the Temple. Her personal qualities of generosity and compassion made her very popular with the membership. Her departure posed a threat to Rev. Jones' absolute control. Rev. Jones delivered a number of public tirades against her. He said that her kindness was faked and that she was a C.I.A. agent. He swore that he would never return her son to her.

15. I am informed that Rev. Jones believed that he would be able to stop Timothy Stoen, husband of Grace Stoen and father of John Victor Stoen, from speaking against the Temple as long as the child was being held in Guyana. Timothy Stoen, a former Assistant District Attorney in Mendocino and San Francisco counties, had been one of Rev. Jones' most trusted advisors. It was rumored that Stoen was critical of the use of physical force and other forms of intimidation against Temple members. I am further informed that Rev. Jones believed that a public statement by Timothy Stoen would increase the tarnish on his public image.

16. When the Temple lost track of Timothy Stoen, I was assigned to track him down and offer him a large sum of money in return for his silence. Initially, I was to offer him $5,000. I was authorized to pay him up to $10,000. I was not able to locate him and did not see him again until on or about October 6, 1977. On that date, the Temple received information that he would be joining Grace in a San Francisco Superior Court action to determine the custody of John. I was one of a group of Temple members assigned to meet him outside the court and attempt to intimidate him to prevent him from going inside.

17. The September, 1977 crisis concerning John Stoen reached major proportions. The radio messages from Guyana were frenzied and hysterical. One morning, Terry J. Buford, public relations advisor to Rev. Jones, and myself were instructed to place a telephone call to a high-ranking Guyanese official who was visiting the United States and deliver the following threat: unless the government of Guyana took immediate steps to stall the Guyanese court action regarding John Stoen's custody, the entire population of Jonestown would extinguish itself in a mass suicide by 5:30 P.M. that day. I was later informed that Temple members in Guyana placed similar calls to other Guyanese officials.

18. We later received radio communication to the effect that the court case had been stalled and that the suicide threat was called off.

19. I arrived in Guyana in December, 1977. I spent a week in Georgetown and then, pursuant to orders, traveled to Jonestown.

20. Conditions at Jonestown were even worse than I had feared they would be. The settlement was swarming with armed guards. No one was permitted to leave unless on a special assignment and these assignments were given only to the most trusted. We were allowed to associate with Guyanese people only while on a "mission".

21. The vast majority of the Temple members were required to work in the fields from 7 A.M. to 6 P.M. six days per week and on Sunday from 7 A.M. to 2 P.M. We were allowed one hour for lunch. Most of this hour was

spent walking back to lunch and standing in line for our food. Taking any other breaks during the workday was severely frowned upon.

22. The food was woefully inadequate. There was rice for breakfast, rice water soup for lunch, and rice and beans for dinner. On Sunday, we each received an egg and a cookie. Two or three times a week we had vegetables. Some very weak and elderly members received one egg per day. However, the food did improve markedly on the few occasions when there were outside visitors.

23. In contrast, Rev. Jones, claiming problems with his blood sugar, dined separately and ate meat regularly. He had his own refrigerator which was stocked with food. The two women with whom he resided, Maria Katsaris and Carolyn Layton, and the two small boys who lived with him, Kimo Prokes and John Stoen, dined with the membership. However, they were in much better physical shape than everyone else since they were also allowed to eat the food in Rev. Jones' refrigerator.

24. In February, 1978, conditions had become so bad that half of Jonestown was ill with severe diarrhea and high fevers. I was seriously ill for two weeks. Like most of the other sick people, I was not given any nourishing foods to help recover. I was given water and a tea drink until I was well enough to return to the basic rice and beans diet.

25. As the former financial secretary, I was aware that the Temple received over $65,000 in Social Security checks per month. It made me angry to see that only a fraction of the income of the senior citizens in the care of the Temple was being used for their benefit. Some of the money was being used to build a settlement that would earn Rev. Jones the place in history with which he was so obsessed. The balance was being held in "reserve". Although I felt terrible about what was happening, I was afraid to say anything because I knew that anyone with a differing opinion gained the wrath of Jones and other members.

26. Rev. Jones' thoughts were made known to the population of Jonestown by means of broadcasts over the

loudspeaker system. He broadcast an average of six hours
per day. When the Reverend was particularly agitated, he
would broadcast for hours on end. He would talk on and
on while we worked in the fields or tried to sleep. In
addition to the daily broadcasts, there were marathon
meetings six nights per week.

27. The tenor of the broadcasts revealed that Rev.
Jones' paranoia had reached an all-time high. He was
irate at the light in which he had been portrayed by the
media. He felt that as a consequence of having been
ridiculed and maligned, he would be denied a place in
history. His obsession with his place in history was
maniacal. When pondering the loss of what he considered
his rightful place in history, he would grow despondent
and say that all was lost.

28. Visitors were infrequently permitted access to
Jonestown. The entire community was required to put on
a performance when a visitor arrived. Before the visitor
arrived, Rev. Jones would instruct us on the image we
were to project. The workday would be shortened. The
food would be better. Sometimes there would be music
and dancing. Aside from these performances, there was
little joy or hope in any of our lives. An air of
despondency prevailed.

29. There was constant talk of death. In the early days
of the People's Temple, general rhetoric about dying for
principles was sometimes heard. In Jonestown, the
concept of mass suicide for socialism arose. Because our
lives were so wretched anyway and because we were so
afraid to contradict Rev. Jones, the concept was not
challenged.

30. An event which transpired shortly after I reached
Jonestown convinced me that Rev. Jones had sufficient
control over the minds of the residents that it would be
possible for him to effect a mass suicide.

31. At least once a week, Rev. Jones would declare a
"white night", or state of emergency. The entire
population of Jonestown would be awakened by blaring
sirens. Designated persons, approximately fifty in
number, would arm themselves with rifles, move from

cabin to cabin, and make certain that all members were responding. A mass meeting would ensue. Frequently during these crises, we would be told that the jungle was swarming with mercenaries and that death could be expected at any minute.

32. During one "white night", we were informed that our situation had become hopeless and that the only course of action open to us was a mass suicide for the glory of socialism. We were told that we would be tortured by mercenaries if we were taken alive. Everyone, including the children, was told to line up. As we passed through the line, we were given a small glass of red liquid to drink. We were told that the liquid contained poison and that we would die within 45 minutes. We all did as we were told. When the time came when we should have dropped dead, Rev. Jones explained that the poison was not real and that we had just been through a loyalty test. He warned us that the time was not far off when it would become necessary for us to die by our own hands.

33. Life at Jonestown was so miserable and the physical pain of exhaustion was so great that this event was not traumatic for me. I had become indifferent as to whether I lived or died.

34. During another "white night", I watched Carolyn Layton, my former sister-in-law, give sleeping pills to two young children in her care, John Victor Stoen and Kimo Prokes, her own son. Carolyn said to me that Rev. Jones had told her that everyone was going to have to die that night. She said that she would probably have to shoot John and Kimo and that it would be easier for them if she did it while they were asleep.

35. In April, 1978, I was reassigned to Georgetown. I became determined to escape or die trying. I surreptitiously contacted my sister, who wired me a plane ticket. After I received the ticket, I sought the assistance of the United States Embassy in arranging to leave Guyana. Rev. Jones had instructed us that he had a spy working in the United States Embassy and that he would know if anyone went to the embassy for help. For this reason, I was very fearful.

36. I am most grateful to the United States government and Richard McCoy and Daniel Weber; in particular, for the assistance they gave me. However, the efforts made to investigate conditions in Jonestown are inadequate for the following reasons. The infrequent visits are always announced and arranged. Acting in fear for their lives, Temple members respond as they are told. The members appear to speak freely to American representatives, but in fact they are drilled thoroughly prior to each visit on what questions to expect and how to respond. Members are afraid of retaliation if they speak their true feelings in public.

37. On behalf of the population of Jonestown, I urge that the United States Government take adequate steps to safeguard their rights. I believe that their lives are in danger.

I declare under penalty of perjury that the foregoing is true and correct, except as to those matters stated on information and belief and as to those I believe them to be true.

Executed this 15 day of June, 1978 at San Francisco, California.

DEBORAH LAYTON BLAKEY

APPENDIX E

November 1, 1978

John R. Burke
American Ambassador
American Embassy
Georgetown, Guyana
South America

Dear Mr. Ambassador:

This will confirm earlier reports you have received regarding a proposed congressional delegation trip to Guyana. Congressman Ed Derwinski and I will arrive on November 14 in Georgetown and wish to review with you and other officials the agricultural commune operated by Rev. Jim Jones and the People's Temple. I look forward to meeting with you.

Following is the text of a telegram I am sending to Rev. Jones:

In recent months my office has been visited by constituents who are relatives of members of your church and who expressed anxiety about mothers and fathers, sons and daughters, brothers and sisters who have elected to assist you in the development of your church in Guyana.

I have listened to others who have told me that such concerns are exaggerated. They have been supportive of your church and your work. Your effort, involving so many Americans from a single U.S. geographic location is unique. In an effort to be responsive to these constituents with differing perspectives and to learn more about your church and its work, I intend to visit Guyana and talk with appropriate government officials. I do so as a part of my assigned responsibilities as a Member of the

House Committee on International Relations. Congressman Ed Derwinski (R-Ill), also a member of the committee and staff members of the committee will be accompanying me.

While we are in Guyana, I have asked our Ambassador, John Burke, to make arrangements for transportation to visit your church and agricultural station at Jonestown. It goes without saying that I am most interested in a visit to Jonestown, and would appreciate whatever courtesies you can extend to our Congressional delegation.

Please consider this letter to be an open and honest request to you for information about your work which has been the center of your life and purpose for so many years. In the interest of simplifying communications, it will only be necessary for you to respond to Ambassador John R. Burke at the American Embassy in Georgetown. Since the details of our trip are still being arranged, I am sure the Ambassador and his staff will be able to keep you informed.

I look forward to talking with you either in Jonestown or Georgetown.

                              Sincerely yours,

                              LEO J. RYAN
                              Member of Congress

CC: Congressman Derwinski
     John J. Brady, Jr. Chief of Staff
     International Relations Committee
     James Schollaert

November 1, 1978

Reverend Jim Jones
People's Temple
Box 893
Mission Village, Guyana
South America

Dear Rev. Jones:

In recent months my office has been visited by
constituents who are relatives of members of your church
and who expressed anxiety about mothers and fathers,
sons and daughters, brothers and sisters who have elected
to assist you in the development of your church in
Guyana.

I have listened to others who have told me that such
concerns are exaggerated. They have been supportive of
your church and your work. Your effort, involving so
many Americans from a single U.S. geographic location
is unique. In an effort to be responsive to these
constituents with differing perspectives and to learn more
about your church and its work, I intend to visit Guyana
and talk with appropriate government officials. I do so as
a part of my assigned responsibilities as a Member of the
House Committee on International Relations. Congressman Ed Derwinski (R-Ill), also a member of the
committee and staff members of the committee will be
accompanying me.

While we are in Guyana, I have asked our Ambassador, John Burke, to make arrangements for transportation to visit your church and agricultural station at Jonestown. It goes without saying that I am most interested in a
visit to Jonestown, and would appreciate whatever
courtesies you can extend to our Congressional delegation.

Please consider this letter to be an open and honest request to you for information about your work which has been the center of your life and purpose for so many years. In the interest of simplifying communications, it will only be necessary for you to respond to Ambassador John R. Burke at the American Embassy in Georgetown. Since the details of our trip are still being arranged, I am sure the Ambassador and his staff will be able to keep you informed.

I look forward to talking with you either in Jonestown or Georgetown.

Sincerely yours,

LEO J. RYAN
Member of Congress

CC: Congressman Derwinski
    John J. Brady, Jr., Chief of Staff
    International Relations Committee
    James Schollaert

Member of the Bar
of the State of New York

1177 Central Avenue
Memphis, Tennessee 38104
901 726-1800

Nov. 6, 1978

Congressman Leo J. Ryan
1720 South Amphlett Blvd.
Suite 219
San Mateo, California 94402

Dear Congressman Ryan:

It is my understanding that you and another member
of Congress and possibly two members of the staff of the
International Relations Committee of the U.S. House of
Representatives wish to visit Jonestown, Guyana due to
complaints that have been made about the project there.
It is also my understanding that you or members of the
staff of the Committee have been briefed by persons
hostile to the People's Temple and the project in
Jonestown. It would seem to me both fair and appropriate for you to seek information from the other side as well
before embarking upon a trip to Jonestown. Since I
represent the People's Temple in various matters, I should
be happy to meet with you and tell you of my experiences
in Jonestown and with Jim Jones and with the People's
Temple.

I have been informed that you wish to tour Jonestown
during the middle of November. My client as asked that I
be present while you make that tour. It seems entirely
appropriate and proper that I should be there on that
occasion. Accordingly, I placed a telephone call to your
San Mateo office at 9 A.M. on Friday, November 3, 1978
to make arrangements for your trip to Jonestown and to
discuss the entire matter with you. Your aide stated that
you would return my telephone call but I have not as yet

heard directly from you. However, I did receive a telephone call from Jim Schollaert who told me that he was a member of the Committee's staff. I informed him that I would be engaged during the middle of November in that I would be representing several witnesses who were to appear in public testimony before the House Select Committee on Assassinations in Washington, D.C. from the middle until the end of November. I suggested to Mr. Schollaert that if you called me we could no doubt work out a date which would be satisfactory to all of us.

You should understand that Jonestown is a private community and that while they appear willing to host your visit there under certain circumstances, courtesy requires that arrangements be made in advance of your visit. For example: there are no hotels or restaurants in the area and you would be the guest of the community during your entire visit. The people of Jonestown have expressed a willingness to care for your needs and the needs of your staff and associates but they suggest, and I certainly agree, that a date which would be convenient to all of us should be arrived at through discussion.

You should be informed that various agencies of the U.S. Government have somewhat consistently oppressed the People's Temple and sought to interfere with the People's Temple, a religious institution. I am now exploring that matter fully in order to bring an action against those agencies of the U.S. Government that have violated the rights of my client. Some of the members of the People's Temple have had to flee from the U.S. in order to experience a fuller opportunity to enjoy rights which were not available to them within the U.S. You should know that two different countries, neither one of which has entirely friendly relations with the U.S., have offered refuge to the 1200 Americans now residing in Jonestown. Thus far the People's Temple has not accepted either of those offers but it is their position that if religious persecution continues and if it is furthered through a witch hunt conducted by any branch of the U.S. Government, that they will be constrained to consider accepting either of the offers. You may judge, therefore, the important consequences which may flow from further persecution of People's Temple and which might very well result in the creation of a most embarrassing situation for the U.S. Government.

I hope that this matter can be resolved in an amicable fashion and I continue to wait for a telephone call from you so that we may discuss this matter more fully.

Very truly yours,

Mark Lane

ML:br
CC: Jean Brown

COMMITTEES:
GOVERNMENT OPERATIONS

CHAIRMAN:
ENVIRONMENT, ENERGY AND
NATURAL RESOURCES
GOVERNMENT INFORMATION AND
INDIVIDUAL RIGHTS
INTERNATIONAL RELATIONS

INTERNATIONAL ORGANIZATIONS
INTERNATIONAL OPERATIONS
POST OFFICE AND
CIVIL SERVICE
POSTAL OPERATIONS AND SERVICES
CENSUS AND POPULATION

LEO J. RYAN, M.C.
11TH DISTRICT, CALIFORNIA

PLEASE REPLY TO:
WASHINGTON OFFICE: □
137 CANNON HOUSE OFFICE BUILDING
WASHINGTON, D.C. 20515
(202) 225-3531

DISTRICT OFFICE: □
1720 SOUTH AMPHLETT BLVD.
SUITE 219
SAN MATEO, CALIFORNIA 94402
(415) 349-1976

Congress of the United States
House of Representatives
Washington, D.C. 20515

November 10, 1978

Mr. Mark Lane
Attorney at Law
1177 Central Ave.
Memphis, Tenn. 38104

Dear Mr. Lane:

I am in receipt of your letter regarding the proposed visit of a delegation from the House International Relations Committee to the nation of Guyana. While I am pleased to have your offer of assistance to the Committee on behalf of the People's Temple at Jonestown I must respectfully dissent from certain assumptions which were apparent in your letter.

First, the Committee and its staff, as a matter of policy and standard practice, works through our Embassy and the government of the nation which it visits. Second, it is my policy, when I am a delegation Chairman conducting inquiries at home or abroad, to deal with the principals in a given situation. To that end, I sent a telegram on November 1 to Mr. Jim Jones asking for his cooperation in a matter affecting the personal lives of an unknown but large number of U.S. citizens, who are presently residing on his property in Jonestown and in Georgetown. He has not yet replied, but I presume he is in touch with the American Embassy and Ambassador John Burke about this inquiry. It is for this reason that I asked Mr. James Schollaert, as an attorney on the staff of the Committee, to respond to your telephone inquiry, to which you make reference.

I regret that you will not be able to be in Guyana, this next week, but I understand that Mr. Jones has other legal counsel available in the event he feels such counsel is necessary. In a situation where the Committee schedule does not coincide with your own personal schedule, I must obviously resolve such a conflict for the United States House of Representatives. I hope that you will understand.

I am also interested in your statement that "various agencies of the U.S. Government have somewhat consistently oppressed the People's Temple." Any such assumption with regard to our Committee is grossly in error. I am interested in locating and talking to certain persons in that community whose mothers, fathers, brothers, sisters, husbands and wives have asked me to inquire on their behalf.

It is true that most of the comments I have heard from relatives are negative, but that is precisely the purpose of this inquiry. Rather than take the word of relatives who can be presumed to be under some emotional bias, I intend to go to the source and to allow those "on the other side" the opportunity to speak in their own behalf. In this case, I have offered Mr. Jones and his supporters the full opportunity to speak for themselves. I presume they will accept such an offer. It is made with the full intention of allowing any and all to speak for the record.

I am at a loss to understand the references on the second page of your letter to members of Mr. Jones' group who have had to "flee from the United States to enjoy their freedom." I certainly hope such persons will be available to give such testimony to support your comment.

I am even more puzzled by your further vague references to one or two other countries that have offered "refuge" to the 1200 Americans in Jonestown. Am I to understand, then, that all 1200 have already been asked if they would be willing to travel to yet another country and begin their lives, under what must already be difficult conditions at best? Perhaps we can learn more about that after we arrive.

Finally, Mr. Lane, I am truly disappointed with your use of the phrase "witch hunt" in connection with an open and honest inquiry of the United States House of Representatives into the welfare of American citizens presently living in Jonestown. The committee asks no more of Mr. Jones than any parent does whose son or daughter is away at school or whose mother or father resides in a distant convalescent home or hospital.

No "persecution", as you put it, is intended, Mr. Lane. But your vague reference to the "the creation of the most embarrassing situation for the American government" does not impress me at all. If the comment is intended as a threat, I believe it reveals more than may have been intended. I presume Mr. Jones would not be supportive of such a comment.

The Committee does intend to leave as scheduled. It does intend to discuss the whereabouts, living conditions and general welfare of the 1200 Americans you refer to, with our Embassy, with the officials of the nation of Guyana and of course, we hope, with Mr. Jones as the leader of the group. We ask for and hope for the cooperation of all. I, too, hope that the inquiry can move ahead in an amicable fashion.

Sincerely yours,

LEO J. RYAN
Member of Congress

LJR/cg

CC: Reverend Jim Jones

Foreign Minister of Guyana

Prime Minister of Guyana

Ambassador Laurence Mann of Guyana

Ambassador John Burke of United States

Assistant Secretary of State
for Latin American Affairs

APPENDIX F

JIM JONES WRITES:
Perspectives From Guyana

The warm, gentle tradewinds have come up and the glow of the evening is subsiding quickly into the clear, star-filled night. There is such peace here. There can't be anything so fulfilling anywhere as living this communal life. We watered the garden today. We grouped into bucket brigades to haul water to a two-and-a-half acre plot where we are experimenting with a North American crop. We sang and laughed and joked the whole time, and in the spirit of joy in our accomplishment, urged each other on to a faster pace. We had the whole job done in two hours. I love to work. I was at the beginning of the line, bringing spring water up out of the well that brims full no matter how much we take from it. One who leads is also one who works. And working together this way, we are making the land produce faster than we can clear it.

I work in the fields whenever I can—whenever I am not helping coordinate the defense against the attacks on us in the United States. It strikes me as immensely sad that the vast majority of people submit to the regimentation and extreme tension of a highly technological society. They pay such a high price in strokes, hypertension, physical diseases and mental stress. And yet those who dare to live for high ideals rather than the mediocrity, apathy and indifference that are the order of the day, become the objects of vindictive harrassment.

Cooperative living provides such security. It provides the structure to see that everyone's needs are met. It maximizes everyone's own individual creativity and allows time for pursuit of individual interests. We have classes in rugmaking, weaving, tanning hide, canning, and myriad academic subjects. Seniors and youth alike are learning every type of craft, carpentry, welding, electrical work and even medicine. We have the best nutrition and a very high level of preventive medicine. Each resident has a blood pressure and TPR test (temperature, pulse and respiration) every week.

We enjoy every type of organized sport and recreational games. Musical talents and arts are flourishing. We share every joy and every need. Our lives are secure and rich with variety and growth and expanding knowledge.

What kind of security can money buy to compare to this? I cannot help thinking about someone like Howard Hughes—one of the richest men in the world who died of neglect and lack of proper medical attention. Or John Paul Getty, a billionaire who refused to pay a ransom for his own grandson and kept payphones in his mansions. When we had a nursing home years ago in the Midwest, a well-to-do gentleman was on his deathbed; his relatives started fighting over his handkerchief and bedside belongings the minute he lost consciousness. I was sure the failing man was hearing them bicker. A nursing assistant who was present at the time, Mary Tschetter, had to ask them to leave the room. Carrie Langston, a member of our church, worked for years taking care of very wealthy elderly people, and said that sometimes, even before they passed, their families came in and stripped their homes of all their possessions.

Here, even though we are under the financial burden of developing this agricultural project, we paid for cosmetic surgery for one of our members whose appearance was marred from birth. We could hardly afford to do this, but her psychological development was being hampered, and to us, human values are more important than material things. Surely living for oneself, amassing individual wealth or fighting to stay on top of the pack is no way to live. Your personality and your worth become defined by what you own rather than by what you are or can do for others. When you are without ideals, you live alone and die rejected.

We have got to find a way to share the wealth of the world more equitably. It seems unless America learns this, she will meet as tormented an end as the multi-millionaires she has spawned. In a very real sense, we came here to avoid contributing to the destruction which the country of our birth continues to inflict on less prosperous nations. How can one live free of guilt when one's resources go to sponsor the kind of atrocity I recently read about that took place in Rhodesia? A child was forced to beat his own father, a Black African leader, on the privates until they were severed from his body. The father died from the beating. Several of the persons directing the atrocity were members of the U.S. military, one of them a major. How can individual Americans consider themselves blameless when their money, through agencies like the International Monetary Fund, is used to destabilize popularly elected governments such as in Portugal? Just America's past sins alone should cause one to feel guilt. Here we have the clean feeling that we are not contributing to this kind of abuse of power. Perhaps people of conscience in America can challenge such policies privately, but how can you avoid the feeling that you're compromising what you stand for?

I will be back one day. But just as others who have been courageous enough to stand up and speak their minds in America have paid the final price—whether revolutionary as the first Americans who believed in liberty or death, or whether non-violent, like Martin Luther King—I also expect to die for my beliefs. And in these days you don't have to be as great a man as Martin Luther King to die for taking a stand.

For all those who would be concerned about our eventual fate, you should know we have found fulfillment. We have gotten ourselves together. We share every moment. When I see the seniors happy and productive, when I see the children gather to perform a play, I know we have lived. Life without principle is devoid of meaning. We have tasted life based on principle and now have no desire to ever live otherwise again. You do not know what happiness is until you have lived up to your

highest. You should come. Often I wish I could be there
with you, but I had no choice. They were going to harm
youngsters and seniors, and I am a leader who could not
leave one soul who looks to me for guidance to that fate. I
feel it is my duty to protect them from senseless
destruction. We were being set up by provocateurs. I am
not about to let us be used as an excuse to bring hardship
down on the people of the United States.

Now there is peace. For the seniors there is freedom
from loneliness and the agony of racism. For the children,
as simple a relief as no more bedwetting or bad dreams.
We have found security and fulfillment in collectivism,
and we can help build a peaceful agricultural nation.

I know some of you there will suffer for the ideas you
now guard carefully behind closed doors. One civil rights
leader has called to tell us the same writers who were after
us have come around to check on him. But when you have
stood up for your rights, when you have done all you can
for oppressed people, there is no longer any fear. I know
well that I am not as articulate as Martin Luther King, Jr.,
Malcolm X, or Eugene V. Debs, but my head is on
straight and I am well-trained for battle. No one could be
more fearless or principled. Neither my colleagues nor I
are any longer caught up in the opiate of religion nor the
narcissistic indulgences of trying to keep ourselves young.
And yet, in the balmy tropical sun and gentle breezes, we
have shed the physical afflictions of the dog-eat-dog
world. Arthritis, diabetes, kidney ailments, hypertension—they have been reduced to almost nothing
here.

We have found a healthy and meaningful existence.
There are high relationships here, ones that do not come
just out of sex, but by sharing and living the highest ideals.
We have passed beyond alienation and have found a way
of living that nurtures trust—one that could speak to a
society grown cynical and cold.

* * * * *

It is obvious someone or some group wants to
denigrate what is going on here. A long time ago a high-

ranking official had told us we would be having difficulty in the future. We did not pay much attention at the time, but now it all fits together like pieces to a puzzle. A powerful agency he had mentioned was, as crazy as it sounds, threatened because we were too effective at organizing people of all races to work together. In the eventuality of economic crisis, it was thought we would have too much organizing potential among the economically deprived of all races. Organization for survival of the poor was not on their agenda.

He told us also that there were individuals planted in our ranks who would try to promote terrorist activities. When this in fact happened, we were reluctant to credit their motives to deceit, and we regarded them as ignorant and youthful fanatics. But now, when we see these same ones who tried to steer us on a violent course being picked up and dignified by some of the media—with no thought given to challenging their word with as much as a lie detector test—it is obvious that the official's warning was correct. We had provocateurs in our midst.

There have been so many obstructions thrown in our way throughout the years. We had thought several years ago to do a documentary film about our work in alternatives to drug addiction, anti-social behavior, and violence. The next morning, after having discussed our ideas over the telephone, we received a phone call from an "agent" for some "movie producer" offering a face-to-face meeting for a promising contract. When we checked through the police to locate the source of the call, we found an office building with no such company where someone could have easily been waylaid in a corridor. It is difficult to convey this kind of intrigue that has followed us in a few short lines—there have been very sophisticated attempts to set me up like this. There have been more death threats and attempted frame-ups than I can begin to count, not only on me and my family, but also on many of the church leaders.

Even if the powerful were to succeed in smearing and destroying this one voice for racial and economic justice, it is ridiculous that they underestimate the intelligence of the general public, the little man I have represented who had no voice. Someone will *always* rise up to speak again. People are beginning to see through the overkill that has been perpetrated against civil rights leaders, and I believe the people will prevail.

* * * * *